D1520650

Racism in American Popular Media

Racism in American Popular Media

From Aunt Jemima to the Frito Bandito

BRIAN D. BEHNKEN AND
GREGORY D. SMITHERS

Racism in American Institutions
Brian D. Behnken, Series Editor

 PRAEGER

AN IMPRINT OF ABC-CLIO, LLC
Santa Barbara, California • Denver, Colorado • Oxford, England

Library of Congress Cataloging-in-Publication Data

Behnken, Brian D.
   Racism in American popular media : from Aunt Jemima to the Frito Bandito / Brian D. Behnken and Gregory D. Smithers.
       pages cm. — (Racism in American institutions)
   Includes bibliographical references and index.
   ISBN 978-1-4408-2976-5 (hardback)   ISBN 978-1-4408-2977-2 (ebook)
   1. Mass media and race relations—United States.   2. Racism in mass media—United States.   3. Mass media and minorities—United States.
I. Smithers, Gregory D., 1974–   II. Title.
   P94.5.M552U625 2015
   305.8—dc23   2014042819

ISBN: 978-1-4408-2976-5
EISBN: 978-1-4408-2977-2

19 18 17 16 15   1 2 3 4 5

This book is also available on the World Wide Web as an eBook.
Visit www.abc-clio.com for details.

Praeger
An Imprint of ABC-CLIO, LLC

ABC-CLIO, LLC
130 Cremona Drive, P.O. Box 1911
Santa Barbara, California 93116-1911

This book is printed on acid-free paper ∞

Manufactured in the United States of America

Contents

Series Foreword

Racism in American Popular Media: From Aunt Jemima to the Frito Bandito is the first book to be published in Praeger Publisher's series, Racism in American Institutions (RAI), that examines the ways in which racism has become institutionalized in the media. The RAI series focuses on the ways in which racism has become, and remains, a part of the fabric of many American institutions. For example, while the United States may have done away with overtly racist acts such as extralegal lynching, racism still affects many of America's established institutions from public schools to corporate offices. Schools may not be legally segregated, and yet many districts are not integrated. While the media discarded many of its most racist practices and characters years ago, examples of black people depicted as criminals, Latinos depicted as lazy, or Native Americans depicted as disappearing savages remain with us. This open-ended series of works examines the problem of racism in established American institutions. Each book in the RAI series traces the prevalence of racism within a particular institution throughout the history of the United States and explores the problem in that institution today, looking at ways in which the institution has attempted to rectify racism, but also the ways in which it has not.

In *Racism in American Popular Media*, RAI series editor Brian D. Behnken has teamed up with historian Gregory D. Smithers to offer a broad-ranging account of racism in the media. We contend that racism not only became institutionalized in the popular media, but that racist caricatures and stereotypical depictions were some of the earliest, and most popular, features of the print (both fiction and nonfiction), advertising, and motion picture (later cartoons and television) industries. One need look no further than early fiction and nonfiction to see examples of works that explored racial difference and always cast persons of color in a negative light. These include popular racist nonfiction accounts such as Charles Carroll's *The Negro, A Beast* and popular fictional works such as Sax Rohmer's *The Insidious Dr. Fu-Manchu*. Advertisers learned quickly that race and racism helped sell products, so featuring a mammy figure like Aunt Jemima on a box of ready-to-make pancake mix made sense to advertisers. In other cases products used gross names on their labels as well, from "Nigger Head Stove Polish" to "Sambo Watermelon." Hollywood also participated in this racism, producing numerous early films focusing on race and racism, from the well-known *Birth of a Nation* to the now largely forgotten *Broncho Billy and The Greaser*. Eventually ethnic communities grew tired of this treatment and demanded that the media create more positive portrayals of minorities. This took the form of civil rights campaigns, from the National Association for the Advancement of Colored Peoples protests against *Birth of a Nation* to the Mexican American community's protests of the "Frito Bandito" character.

Brian D. Behnken and Gregory D. Smithers are well positioned to explore the history of racism in the popular media. Both are historians by training who have lengthy publication records that have examined racism, popular culture, and civil rights activism within a multidisciplinary framework. *Racism in American Popular Media* builds on their expertise, fleshing out not only the long history of racism in the popular media, but also examining the ways in which people of color have challenged this racism.

Brian D. Behnken
Iowa State University
Ames, Iowa

Introduction

At the dawn of the twenty-first century, popular forms of media surround us, permeating almost every waking moment of our lives. Popular media has proliferated to such an extent that scholars have scrambled over the past generation to make sense of it all. Detailed analyses by cultural historians and media studies experts have identified a dizzying array of popular media, from emerging niche cultures involving Internet sites like YouTube or Facebook to massive content deliverers such as Netflix and Amazon Prime, from books or newsmagazines to what are now seen as "traditional" pop culture formats such as film and television.[1]

Popular media, however, has a long history in North America that stretches farther back in time than the advent of moving pictures, television, and the Internet. Native Americans, for example, expressed their own forms of popular culture in their daily routines, songs, ceremonies, and stories, long before Africans and Europeans arrived in the Americas. When African and European peoples did begin arriving in the "New World" during the fifteenth and sixteenth centuries, they brought with them their own ideas, cultures, and forms of expression. In what became the United States, the intertwining of Native American, African, and European lives brought different cultures and belief systems together; some of these amalgamated to produce distinctively American forms of expression and cultural practices. Most significantly, the process of cultural retention, amalgamation, and reinvention occurred in colonial contexts in which social, political, economic, and military power was negotiated and/or fought over. That the British, and subsequently the Anglo-Americans, prevailed in stamping their vision of social and cultural order on the geographical and human landscape of North America provides us with a revealing entry point with which to study race and racism in American popular media during the nineteenth and twentieth centuries.

Given that race and racism have been critical organizing principles in the colonial and subsequent national histories of North America, this book provides an introduction into the complexities of race and racism in the popular media. There exist myriad forms of popular media, but for purposes of clarity and concision we have chosen to focus on four main areas: fictional and nonfictional books, advertising, movies, and cartoons. These forms of media were among the most ubiquitous and widely consumed in the United States during the nineteenth and twentieth centuries. Our accounts and analysis of the content of these popular media forms are designed to provide the reader with an overview of the major ideas and cultural expressions about race and racism that circulated through American popular culture. It is also our intention that the following chapters will spark discussion and further analysis of the nature, types, and impacts of race and racism in American popular media.[2]

Race and racism punctuated virtually all facets of American life during the nineteenth and twentieth centuries. This proved especially true for the American entertainment industry, which became both larger and increasingly specialized over the two centuries discussed in this book. In other words, popular forms of media—from books to advertisements—became institutionally embedded in American cultural life. In the constantly changing entertainment and advertising industries that the following chapters introduce readers to, the representation of racist and sexist beliefs and behaviors was both replicated and made anew with each new book, film, advertisement, and/or cartoon. Through these mediums, Americans were exposed to visual and aural cues that naturalized white supremacy at the expense of African Americans, Native Americans, Mexican Americans and other Latinos, and people of Asian ancestry.[3]

Race and racism became such a central part of popular media during the nineteenth and twentieth centuries that the presence of discriminatory stories or visual representations became naturalized to the point of invisibility. Literature and film scholar Clyde Taylor has made a similar observation in relation to the ubiquity of racism in Hollywood films. Taylor contends that racism was so common in the film industry that it has blinded film critics to the institutionalized nature of discriminatory images. To make his point, Taylor points to how a large cohort of film scholars view early Hollywood classics, such as D. W. Griffith's *Birth of a Nation* (1915), solely in terms of its aesthetic innovations and breakthroughs in cinematography. Film scholars often ignore the racism that characterized this film, explain it away as "unconscious" or as a "product of its time," or frame it as an aberration in an otherwise groundbreaking piece of filmmaking. Treating racism as "passive," to borrow from Taylor, ignores just how pervasive racial (and racist) forms of thinking were in twentieth-century America and how racial ideologies became embedded in the institutional structures of American society.[4]

But what are institutions? Scholars from a range of disciplines—from political science to history—continue to debate the meaning and significance of institutions in our daily lives. For the purposes of our analysis, we have adopted a broad interdisciplinary approach to this subject, defining institutions as those entities that exercise both physical and ideological influences over our lives and that tend to regulate how people think and act. Institutions can come in many forms; they can take on concrete forms, as is the case with the policing of laws or the use of scientific theories. In such cases, an identifiable body—often in the form of a centralized organization such as a government or research university—helps to rank, order, and embed a given set of laws, concepts, or scientific theories in society. Alternatively, institutions and institutional ways of thinking can lack an identifiable physical structure and occupy an abstract or "mental" space in the minds of people. In this case, the institutional influences in society can be more difficult to identify as they often combine a loose conglomeration of ideas, cultural practices, and intergenerational experiences.[5]

Popular media, which some scholars refer to as "mass media," constituted a variety of institutional forms during the nineteenth and twentieth centuries. Everything from newspapers, books (both fiction and nonfiction), movies, and advertisements was widely available to the consuming public and, as such, exercised both "concrete" and "mental" forms of institutional impacts on American society and culture.[6] Over the course of two centuries, the publishing industry, the film and cartoon industries, and the advertising industry were shaped by institutional forces that were both internal and external to their respective operations. Industry standards and practices established in, for example, advertising involved guidelines set from within the industry and, as the twentieth century unfolded, from external forces like government regulators who increasingly made demands on industry insiders to modify the types of images and/or claims that advertisers could make. In these ways, the push and pull of cultural forces within, and from outside, the advertising industry highlights how institutions are far from static, monolithic entities; they are sites of cultural exchange and contestations in which the social order and cultural norms of a society are constantly under negotiation.

These negotiation/contestation processes are often only visible with any degree of clarity in hindsight. These processes are nonetheless important to ensuring that the institutions that exist in a society remain relevant and meaningful to the people they purport to serve. Popular media outlets, such as the filmmaking industry, provide a clear example of how one institution evolved over time to both reflect popular culture and educate audiences. Over the course of the twentieth century, film proved a particularly effective medium through which to shine a mirror on societal conventions, but also to articulate those ideas that remained relatively unclear in their articulation.

This proved to be the case with ideas about race and the expression of different forms of racism. Concepts of racial difference, and the racism they give meaning to, have never been static concepts. Race is an expression of human difference with chameleon-like qualities, a "scavenger ideology" that has evolved (and continues to evolve) over time. During the nineteenth and twentieth centuries, race and racism acquired its social force and cultural meaning through the promiscuous use of religion, politics, history, biology (and science generally), and culture. For many people, race and racism were reductive; certain types of people looked or acted or possessed (or lacked) certain characteristics. Race was based on phenotype—what people looked like or their bloodline or where they came from—that was often linked to ability, intelligence, or social standing. For many white European Americans, nonwhites because of their heritage or phenotype were inferior.

Racism was, and is, the cultural, economic, or social expression of this perception of inferiority. Commonly held tropes about blacks, Latinos, Asian, or Native Americans, themselves generations in the making, gave voice to American—and global—concepts of race. In the popular media, those tropes took the form of oddly or humorously dressed people; characters such as Mammies, Sambos, or Uncle Toms; concepts of Latino laziness or criminality; the perception of duplicity or the untrustworthiness of Asians; and the noble savage, drunken Indian, or warrior savage.

In numerous cases, those archetypical characters were brought to life in advertisements, fictional and nonfictional writing, films, and cartoons. Often white actors portrayed nonwhites, as whites were seen, oddly enough, as the only people legitimately capable of portraying such characters. This perhaps had its genesis in blackface minstrelsy, in which white actors pretended to be blacks for comical purposes. But black people were not the only individuals portrayed in this light: white actors portrayed Asians in yellowface, Mexicans and other Latinos in what we call Latinoface or brownface, and indigenous people in redface. For many nonwhite actors in films and advertisements, as well as cartoon depictions of these stereotypical characters, the only roles available were often ones that approximated the blackface, Latinoface, yellowface, or redface depictions originated by white people. The portrayal of these racist characters by actors of color has come to be known as black-blackface, yellow-yellowface, red-redface, and Latino-Latinoface (or brown-brownface), terms that we use throughout this book.

We explore a number of the most common stereotypical character types, which indeed become so ubiquitous that they were both stereotypical advertising archetypes. These include African Americans as indolent, unintelligent, comical; as Sambos or Mammies; as oddly speaking or dressing. They also include portrayals of Latinos as thieves, bandits, or urban thugs; as lazy; Latinas as sexually hot; as law-breaking border crossers who solely dress in sombreros or serapes. For Native Americans, their depictions were often rooted in their place in North American history. They were either a dying breed of disappearing people or bound to the reservation—or both. They were either drunken or a noble savage; assimilated or a fierce warrior. Asians were shown as unhygienic people who spread disease or as individuals who were perpetually foreign (the same could be said of Native Americans and Latinos). Asians were depicted as being evil or demonic; as wily or sinister; as possessing mystical powers that they used for evil, and occasionally for good.

Many of these archetypes found expression in numerous depictions in advertising, in books, and in movies and cartoons. The Mammy character is a good example, appearing in countless forms from Hattie McDaniel's "Mammy" in *Gone with the Wind* to the unnamed "Mammy Two Shoes" in *Tom and Jerry* cartoons. The Latino/Latina stereotypical characters could be seen in popular forms such as the Cuban fireball and the Mexican border bandit, or in characters such as Zorro or Speedy Gonzales. Asian archetypes found popular expression in books and films focusing on Dr. Fu Manchu—the evil, sinister Asian—or Charlie Chan—the good Asian who uses his mystical powers of deduction to solve crimes. These character types also have their female equivalent in the sinister "dragon lady" and demure "China doll" archetypes. While real-life native peoples, such as Geronimo or Sitting Bull, often were the fodder of writers and moviemakers, the fierce warrior or noble savage also came to light in hundreds of stories and films, especially "cowboys and Indians" movies and books. So often could Americans see such characters, so ubiquitous were they, that these types of characters and the racist baggage that accompanied them became normative for many Americans. Moreover, their ubiquity shows how racist depictions could become institutionalized in the popular media.

In the following chapters we explore all of these archetypes and stereo-typical characters—and more—to demonstrate the prevalence of racism in the popular media. We introduce readers to the ways in which popular fictional and nonfictional books, movies, advertising, and cartoons reflected racist ideologies and gave voice to widely held concepts of human difference. We do this by focusing specifically on media portrayals of African Americans, Native Americans, Asian Americans, and Latinos/Latinas in the nineteenth and long twentieth centuries.

Chapter 1 begins with the earliest, and most prolific, media purveyor of racist beliefs: the publishing industry. Both popular fictional and non-fictional writing first gave voice and lent credence to American racist stereotypes. Nonfictional, pseudoscientific writers, for instance, produced a number of books and studies that attempted to explain human difference and justify racist institutions and practices, such as slavery and segregation. Fictional writers frequently lampooned people of color, making blacks, Latinos, Asians, and Native Americans the butt of jokes, the comedic relief, or the boogymen of countless stories. We argue that popular fiction, bolstered by racist nonfiction, allowed readers to craft mental images based on their broader understanding of the world. Writers created a visual map of the world and its people, giving written clarity and authority to the racism in people's everyday lives.

Chapter 2 examines another of the pioneering media enterprises to capitalize on racism: the advertising industry. Advertisers discovered in the nineteenth century that racism sells. Print ads and, later, radio or television advertisements featured innumerable racist depictions of people of color, from the cigar store Indian to "Nigger Head Stove Polish," from the Jell-O "Chinese baby" (Jell-O made him "vely happy") to the Sanka Mexican, from Aunt Jemima to the Frito Bandito. Advertisers had a ready pool of stereotypical characters from which to draw for their ad campaigns. At the same time, their ads underpinned and gave voice to broader American racial ideals.

Chapter 3 highlights media racism in the American movie industry. Given our discussion of racism in popular fiction and nonfiction and the advertising industry, it hardly seems surprising that many of the first motion pictures dealt with racial and racist themes. The most prolific early racist moviemaker, D. W. Griffith, for example, made films featuring racist depictions of blacks (*Birth of a Nation*), Latinos (*The Greaser's Gauntlet*), and Native Americans (*The Red Man and the Child*). Like advertising, Hollywood discovered that racism was big business. Motion pictures, first in the silent film era and later in the "talkie" period, utilized many of the most familiar racist depictions and caricatures of blacks, Native Americans, Asian Americans, and Latinos, bringing a racist vision to audiences on an unprecedentedly massive scale.

Chapter 4 delves into the racism of cartoons. Animation lent itself to racist caricaturing of people of color, first because black and white hand-drawn animation closely approximated blackface depictions of African Americans and second because cartoons could be surreptitious, offering crude racist humor that because it was a cartoon could seem benign. Because children viewed cartoons, the animation industry, its executives, and creators and directors, all taught American children important lessons about race and racism. In some cases, that racism was more subtle; in the guise of *Tom and Jerry*'s Mammy Two Shoes or Speedy Gonzales cartoon racism seemed funny, rather than offensive. But in many cases animators developed cartoons so distasteful that they were later banned. Whether the racism in cartoons was subtle or overt is somewhat immaterial. Racist depictions were prevalent in cartoons and, more importantly, there were relatively few alternatives that featured characters of color portraying ethnic communities in a positive light.

We conclude with an examination of the ways in which people of color began to resist their negative depictions, especially in film, in cartoons, and in advertising. For instance, while the Frito Bandito helped sell many a corn chip, Mexican-origin people opposed this character, which ultimately ended this particular ad campaign. While blacks, Latinos, Asian Americas, and Native Americans certainly disapproved of their racist depictions in the popular media, the civil rights movements of the 1960s helped initiate a revision of how people of color are portrayed by the media. More recently, Native Americans and their allies have begun protesting the use of Native American likenesses and names, especially in sports, a massive component of the American popular media. *Racism in American Popular Media* thus explores the long history of discrimination in the media, explaining how that racism became institutionalized, but also analyzes how ethnic communities resisted media racism.

Chapter 1

Writing Race

Fictional and popular nonfictional writing has long played a key role in shaping public consciousness about race in the United States. Many of the most popular beliefs about nonwhite people—Native Americans were "doomed" to extinction, African Americans could not be assimilated into American "civilization," and Latinos were "lazy" or prone to criminality—were popularized among the reading public in fictional works.[1] In addition, racist characters such as Mammy, Sambo, and Uncle Tom archetypes; the "noble savage" and fierce Native American warriors; the "lazy Latino"; and the "sinister Oriental" became staples of American writing during the nineteenth and twentieth centuries.[2] Popular characters like Dr. Fu Manchu and Mammy both appeared in popular written works that informed readers about the racial qualities of people of color. It should also be noted that Americans read far more nonfiction in the nineteenth and early twentieth centuries than they do today. Therefore, works categorized as "nonfiction," such as studies of phrenology and eugenics (even though they were almost entirely based on misleading or erroneous data), were read with great interest.[3]

Fictional and popular nonfictional works allowed nineteenth- and twentieth-century readers to visualize a racial map of the world.[4] Authors mapped out a world in which they described people, concepts, and places in ways that conformed to the United States' ever-changing racial understanding of the world. The authors of the nineteenth and twentieth centuries thus gave written, narrative clarity to the unarticulated racial beliefs of readers; in the process, these authors narrated a world dominated by race and racism that ultimately affirmed popular notions about the racial ordering of humankind. As literary scholars Catherine and John Silk observe, "The persistent portrayal of racist ideas in works which reach wide audiences exacerbates the problems of racism and discrimination," something that in turn provides a fertile cultural environment in which racist literature can be produced and reproduced.[5]

In this chapter we provide a broad-ranging overview of the types of popular fictional and nonfictional accounts of racialized groups that over time had important cultural ramifications for how Americans understood race and perceived racial "others." The written articulation of racial and racist viewpoints did not suddenly emerge in the "racial century" between the 1850s and 1950s.[6] But this period was important for the ways in which popular cultural and "scientific" ideas of race meshed to inform the racial worldviews of Americans. Beginning with popular nonfictional writing in the nineteenth century, this chapter is foundational to understanding the representation of race and racism in movies, advertising, and cartoons from the late nineteenth century and well into the twentieth century.

Racist Nonfiction

Popular nonfictional writing proved as influential as fiction in reinforcing racial beliefs and prejudices. Historians and literary scholars have devoted considerable attention to the impact that the authors of eugenic theories, or the idea of selective breeding and forced sterilization among select groups of people in the population, had on American racial thinking during the late nineteenth and early twentieth centuries.[7] American novelists, for instance, used eugenic theories in their stories in various ways. For example, Charlotte Perkins Gilman's *Herland* (1915) was inspired by eugenic theories to postulate the creation of a feminist utopia.[8] Alternatively, Southern novelist Erskine Caldwell—whom one biographer refers to as "the people's writer"—presented readers with an explicitly eugenic piece of fiction at the start of the Great Depression. His *The Bastard* (1929) follows the ill-bred, or "dysgenic," life of Gene Morgan, a "bastard child" whose mother was "a whore in a hoochie-coochie tent."[9] These writers used fictional accounts to advance a real-life social agenda, giving further credence and credibility to eugenic thinking.

Where writers of fiction played a major role in popularizing eugenic ideas, scholars of eugenics have shown how the authors of popular nonfiction helped to give eugenic ideas the appearance of scientific certainty. Authors such as Madison Grant and Lothrop Stoddard used pseudoscientific racial theories to "prove" that black people and other ethno-racial minorities were inferior to whites. Such writers centered their "studies" on the premise that whites were superior to nonwhites. Many of the ideas conveyed by these authors overlapped with popularly held prejudices that were several centuries in the making. As such, they willfully blurred the lines between fact and fiction.[10]

The ability of popular nonfiction writers to blur these lines in the United States has a long history. From nineteenth-century authors with proslavery viewpoints to white supremacists who wrote in support of Jim Crow segregation, scores of writers published books during the nineteenth and twentieth centuries that purported to analyze, categorize, and better explain the "scientific" inferiority of black people. Broadly, this vast corpus of works aimed to highlight the logic behind popularly held notions of African American inferiority. They did this by studying black people through the lens of religion, phrenology, and craniology.[11]

In antebellum America, one of the best examples of this type of analysis from the scientific community comes from the pseudosciences of phrenology. While a number of scholars wrote popular works on these subjects, none was more influential than Samuel George Morton's *Crania Americana*.[12] Morton analyzed a set of human skulls at a time when abolitionist protests against slavery in the South were gaining momentum. While Morton did not write his book with the explicit purpose of defending slavery, the increasingly contentious national debate over slavery did help sales of his book. This proved fortuitous for Morton, as a downturn in the American economy in the late 1830s and the book's hefty price tag of $20 (roughly $500 in today's money) did not bode well for sales. But as historian Ann Fabian observes, "Slavery's defenders ... had cash to spare," and their purchases of the book helped Morton's ideas slowly circulate through American popular culture.[13]

Morton was an early proponent of what ultimately became physical anthropology. His basic assertion was that skull size, shape, and cranial capacity could go far in explaining differences in the human "species." Morton gathered hundreds of skulls from around the world and performed various measurements on them. From the datasets he accumulated, Morton presented the reading public with a number of far-reaching conclusions. The first was theological. In his collection of skulls, Morton included several Egyptian mummies. He found considerable difference between these mummies, concluding that their distinct cranial features, which he equated with ethno-racial difference, indicated that human racial groups were already separate and distinct long before biblical actors such as Noah.[14] According to Morton, this demonstrated that variations among human beings existed in the Bible, if not before biblical time. Thus, there was no single human tree that descended from Adam and Eve; rather, there were multiple lines of humanity, or multiple Adams. This was a profound statement that came to be associated with polygenesis, the theory of human beings deriving from separate origins. Morton further argued that Egyptians were not African or black but white, and that while black people existed in Egypt, they formed a lower caste group in Egyptian society, an interesting finding considering it would seem to be rather difficult to determine societal standing, or lack thereof, by skull size and shape alone.[15]

While Morton was certainly concerned with religion and biblical traditions, he was more concerned with using science to justify racism. In Morton's skull measurements, African descent people always ended up last, while white people came out at the top of his racial hierarchy. For instance, in his study Caucasians had the largest skulls, and hence the biggest brains. Black or African peoples had the smallest skulls in his study. Other groups, such as Asians or Native Americans, had skull sizes that were in between those of white and black people. Examination of Native American crania convinced Morton that indigenous people were equipped with mental qualities that made them proficient at "mimicking" white people, but were essentially "wild and savage" by "nature."[16] Morton also postulated that by measuring skulls using a variety of different techniques he could formulate a basic pattern for determining to which racial group a skull belonged. In fact, Morton believed he could ascertain the "race" of any skull simply by measuring it.

Beyond his data and analysis, Morton included many statements in *Crania Americana* that our modern sensibilities would consider racist and offensive. In detailing the physical qualities of white people, for instance, Morton not only commented on their larger skull size—"the skull is large and oval, and its anterior portion full and elevated. The face is small in proportion to the head, of an oval form, with well-proportioned features. The nasal bones are arched, the chin full, and the teeth vertical."—but added, "this race is distinguished for the facility with which it attains the highest intellectual endowments."[17] These would all seem to be positive features and attributes, not a negative in the entire statement.

Morton's definition of black people, "the Ethiopian race," was far more negative in its tenor. He writes that this "Ethiopian race" is "characterized by a black complexion, and black, woolly hair; the eyes are large and prominent, the nose broad and flat, the lips thick, and the mouth wide: the head is long and narrow, the forehead low, the cheek-bones prominent, the jaws protruding, and the chin small." While his description of whites produced in the mind of nineteenth-century readers a pleasant picture of humanity, his rendering of blacks produced a somewhat Frankenstein-like image of people with bulging eyes and protruding jaws. Morton informed readers that such physical qualities foretold the mental nature of African American people, whom he described as "joyous, flexible, and indolent; while many nations that compose this race present a singular diversity of intellectual character, of which the far extreme is the lowest grade of humanity."[18]

Morton's theories were reductive in nature; that is, they reduced human nature to a series of data points. While sales of Crania Americana were initially slow, Morton's ideas found an appreciative readership in cities such as Charlestown, where his writings helped to underpin seemingly acceptable forms of discrimination under the guise of scientific inquiry. Indeed, Morton became something of a media celebrity, ultimately selling thousands of books and establishing the utility of American science on the global stage. This was important because prior to Morton's Crania Americana, American readers of scientific literature turned to European authors. Morton changed all of that. The connection he made between skull size/brain size and intelligence came at a time when political and cultural debates about slavery and western territorial expansion intensified. The publication of Crania Americana was therefore timely, but it should be noted that scientists today remain divided over the origins and genetic foundations of intelligence. Scientists generally agree, however, that there is little direct connection between skull size or shape and intellectual capacity. Size, for instance, does not account for number of neurons, nor the frequency of neurons firing, nor memory, nor recall, nor even the size of certain sections of the brain: frontal lobe versus parietal lobe, for example.[19] If brain size and shape were as important as Morton claimed, then how can we adequately explain why some individuals with traumatic brain injuries continue to show the same level of cognitive ability as people with, quite literally, double the brain matter?

The larger point that we wish to make here is that Morton's work may well have employed a scientific methodology, but the questions scientists ask, and the answers they draw from their data, have always been informed by the culture in which scientists live as much as the numbers they rely upon. Morton's writings illuminate this point, as his methods used to derive "scientific" conclusions relied on popularly held racial beliefs. For example, Morton sometimes relied on illustrations that reflected the racist perceptions of the artist. Among the illustrations included in Crania Americana were skulls with bullet holes and skulls from mummified, shrunken heads. The drawings of black people were made to appear scientific, but in truth they constituted little more than "scholarly" versions of blackface.[20]

Morton's descriptions of nonwhite peoples reinforced the visual cues. For example, he wrote that "the negro is … the lowest grade of humanity."[21] While Morton's assertion reduced virtually all black people to a lower form of intelligence, his theories had great significance for those racists in American society who hoped to keep black people enslaved. Morton's writings and the racist plates that accompanied *Crania Americana* were serialized in dozens of papers and magazines around the globe, lending the appearance of scientific validation to popular racial prejudices.

While Morton's writings lent scientific credibility to nineteenth-century racism, scores of other writers turned to the Bible to rationalize racial prejudices. Theological writers combined biblical and pseudoscientific theories to explain why God ordained that black people were to be perpetually enslaved. By the antebellum period, religious scholars had for decades justified slavery by using the Bible to frame arguments in support of racial slavery—especially the story of Ham in the book of Genesis, which told of how Ham was cursed by his father Noah and banished to Africa to serve as a perpetual servant.[22] For example, the proslavery theologian Thornton Stringfellow insisted that the "descendants of Ham" had been placed under the care of "Christian masters" in "this land of liberty."[23] And lest anyone question his assessment of slavery's validity, Stringfellow maintained that the "Scriptures" sanction such practices.[24]

Where proslavery theological writers drew on the Old Testament to rationalize the innate inferiority of African Americans, such writers also turned to the New Testament of the Bible to insist that slaves should work diligently and loyally for their masters. Thus, the Old Testament provided proslavery theologians with ample material to justify the "biological" basis for enslaving people of African ancestry, while noting, as the Virginia John Thompson Brown did in a debate about slave emancipation in 1831, that Jesus walked on the earth "to reprove sin. Yet he rebuked not slavery."[25] The New Testament provided the same theological writers with material to go forth and preach about the importance of "personal obedience and reformation" as the cornerstone of a prosperous civilization. Proslavery theological writers interpreted New Testament references to "servants" as "slaves," insisted that the writings of the apostles instructed slaves to be loyal to their masters, and informed masters to act with charity and equanimity toward slaves.[26]

Following the publication of Harriet Beecher Stowe's antislavery novel *Uncle Tom's Cabin* (1852), a slew of novelist and nonfictional writers sympathetic toward slavery contributed to the literary defense of the "peculiar institution." Southern women proved particularly active in writing and publishing novels that defended slavery. Among the most popular of these novels were Mary H. Eastman's *Aunt Phillis's Cabin* (1852), Maria McIntosh's *The Lofty and the Lowly* (1853), and Carline Lee Hentz's *Marcus Warland* (1852) and *The Planter's Northern Bride* (1854). These novels were didactic in nature, providing readers with page after page of biblical justifications for slavery while also explaining to readers how masters kept enslaved families together and nurtured an agricultural utopia.[27]

By the 1850s, then, the volume of proslavery writing had grown and was to continue to grow. The scope of this literature was as broad as the number of volumes being published each year. In addition to female novelists in the South, nonfictional writers such as Josiah Nott and George Gliddon contributed to a growing corpus of pseudoscientific books that justified slavery on explicitly racial grounds. Nott and Gliddon published *Types of Mankind* in 1855, a popularized and commercially successful rendering of Samuel George Morton's theories.[28] The authors of theological justifications for racial slavery also remained active in providing their rationales for the perpetuation of racial slavery. A growing number of proslavery theological authors tied their arguments to a theory known as "theological science." The writers who toyed with such ideas blended concepts about pre-Adamite man, or the belief that human beings existed before the biblical Adam, and polygenesis, the theory of multiple human origins.[29] Blending "Scripture and science," the authors of pre-Adamite tracts attempted to explain the existence of African people and why the descendent of such people were justly enslaved in the Americas.[30] Pre-Adamites argued that some form of humankind had existed before Adam and that these people were God's failed experiments in the creation of human beings. According to the pre-Adamite writers of the antebellum era, God eventually got his/her experiment with the creation of humankind right with Adam and, later, Eve. People of African origin in the minds of these theologians were more akin to monkeys. In fact, according to some authors, they were a type of simian that survived the great flood as a beast on Noah's ark.[31]

The author "Ariel" (a pseudonym for Rev. Buckner Payne) was one of the first theologians to postulate this pre-Adamite theory as it applied to black Americans. His *The Negro: What Is His Ethnological Status* attempted a revision of the historical place of black people across the globe. Payne first restored Ham by debunking both the curse and his blackness. He also distanced blacks from Adam and Eve, noting in a somewhat sarcastic tone, "now, unless it be shown that, from Noah back to Adam and Eve, that in some way this kinky-headed and black-skinned negro is the progeny of Adam and Eve, and which we know can not [sic] be done, then *again* it follows, indubitably, that the negro is not a human being—not being Adam's race." Of course, the reality is much simpler: "the negro must have come out of the ark with the beasts."[32] Payne compared black people to monkeys, both, in his mind, being similar types of beast who survived their time on Noah's ark.[33] Payne/Ariel's ultimate conclusion about African Americans was especially damning. God saved Noah and his family, the only "souls" worthy of salvation of the ark. "The Negro was in the ark; and God thus testifies that he has no soul."[34] As a "beast" with no "soul," Buckner concluded, it was wrong for Americans to consider laws making blacks the social and political equals of whites. To do so would invite God's wrath. The only solution, he asserted, was "*to send him* [the Negro] *back to Africa or re-enslave him.* "[35]

Pre-Adamite thinkers continued to pursue questions about the separate origins of black people well into the twentieth century.[36] In perhaps the most provocatively titled work from the early twentieth century, Professor Charles Carroll, a white supremacist minister from Missouri, published in 1900 *The Negro, a Beast, or in the Image of God.* That book also had a provocative subtitle, "the Negro a beast, but created with articulate speech and hands, that he may be of service to his master—the White man." One need read no further to understand Carroll's point. In his theories, analysis, and interpretation, Carroll did not differ markedly from Ariel. In fact, Carroll summons Ariel's writings to support his own theorizing. However, Carroll's language is far more overt in its racist tenor. Unlike *The Negro: What Is His Ethnological Status*, Carroll also included blackface images. These images served to juxtapose the visage of "the negro" with an image of Jesus, setting up a visual cue for Carroll to ask rhetorically "is the negro in the image of God's son—Christ?" The cone-headed, wooly haired, dark-black-with-bright-lips person pictured next to a blond-haired, blue-eyed Jesus suggested that the answer was unequivocally "no."[37]

Carroll's writings appeared at a time when eugenic ideas were gaining increasing popular and political support in the United States. Carroll's focus on the purported physical dissimilarities of whites and blacks therefore echoed the writings of eugenic authors. He elaborated, for example, on the differences in hair, noses, lips, and skin color between blacks and whites, in addition to asserting the different cranial capacities and brain sizes of these groups. Carroll's writing thus incorporated racist pseudoscience to advance his speculations, while dismissing scientific research that

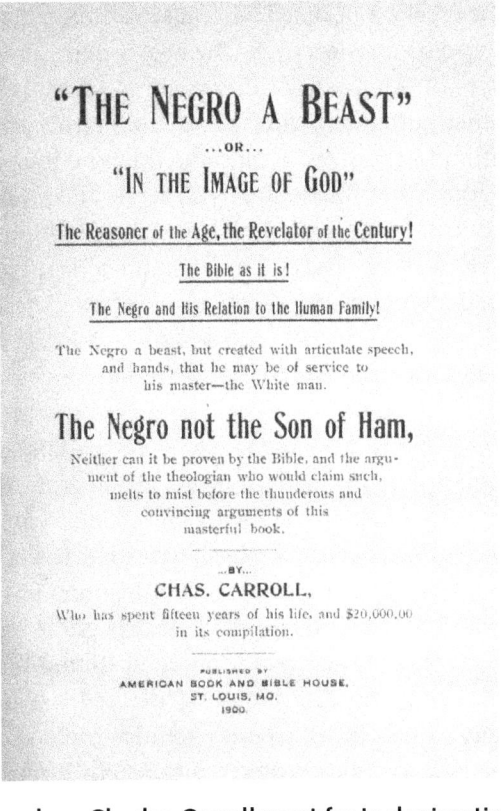

Racist thinkers such as Charles Carroll went far in denigrating black people. Works such as *The Negro, A Beast* also sold well and became a part of a growing publishing industry.

contradicted his racial prejudices. According to Carroll, "It is shown by comparative anatomy that the Negro, from the crown of his woolly head, to the sole of his flat foot, differs in his physical and mental organisms from the White; and that 'just in proportion as he differs from the White, he approximates the lower animals.'"[38]

Like Ariel/Buckner, Carroll devoted much time to disproving Hamitic theory. If black people descended from Noah, then it stood to reason that they descended from Adam and Eve and were, hence, children of God. Pre-Adamitists could not stomach such a thought. Carroll denied Noah the power to curse Ham at all, calling him "an old man 'just coming out of his cups.'"[39] Blacks were not the children of Adam and Eve, rather, "the negro, in common with the rest of the animals, made his appearance upon the earth prior to the creation of man."[40] Because of this, Carroll insisted that black people had no souls. Moreover, "the negro, being an ape, entered the ark with the rest of the animals," further proof in Carroll's mind that black people were neither human nor children of God.[41] This position informed Carroll's opposition to cross-racial unions, which he found abhorrent. He argued that no amount of inbreeding with white folks would give mixed race people a soul. In sum, only white people are children of God and possess a soul. He further asserts that the biblical serpent was "a negro" and that the crucifixion of Jesus was the result of interracial sex and racial amalgamation.[42]

Pre-Adamite writers invented a stable, segmented world, a world utterly different from the real world that was changing around them, but one that still seemed correct and understandable to their readers. In attempting to revise black people's place in the history of the planet, by distancing black people from the curse of Ham and by placing them as simians in the ark, "scholars" like Carroll crafted a biblical narrative that denied African-origin people a soul, the ability to achieve salvation, and, more broadly, their humanity. In the early twentieth century, such beliefs played an important cultural role in justifying racial segregation. Moreover, the writings of Carroll and like-minded authors generated a massive new racist literary machine that helped to validate popular prejudices. Such writers popularized the black-as-monkey stereotype, as our discussions of race in cinema, advertising, and cartoons also highlight. In addition, nonfictional writings by "scholars" like Carroll found expression in the fictional writings of the late nineteenth and early twentieth centuries. The idea of the black-as-monkey stereotype helps to explain why so many Americans recoiled at the idea of interracial sex and/or marriage. Confronting popular fears about interracial sex and marriage, Frances E. W. Harper's novel *Iola Leroy* (1892) featured a white male, Doctor Gresham, proposing marriage to the novel's light-skinned title character. Harper, an African American novelist, had Leroy respond to Dr. Gresham's proposal by stating: "There are barriers between us that I cannot pass. Were you to know them I think you would say the same."[43] African American writers of both fiction and nonfiction thus understood the broad-reaching implications of racism in American society. Therefore, black writers from Harper to black historians like Carter G. Woodson and the historian and sociologist W. E. B. Du Bois did not sit idly during the nineteenth and early twentieth centuries as they deployed their considerable literary skills to debunk racist literature. In addition to critiquing white America's distaste for interracial marriage, books by authors such as the famous African American abolitionist Frederick Douglass demonstrate how not all Americans bought into racist pseudoscientific, pseudo-religious theories about black inferiority, or the supposed separateness of their origins. As Douglass declared in 1884, "God Almighty made but one race."[44]

Racial Fictions

Despite the best efforts of African American authors, the nonfictional and fictional writings of white Americans played an important cultural role in naturalizing antiblack racism in the United States. Where antebellum authors of nonfiction established the "scientific" basis for the separateness and/or racial inferiority of African Americans, or the writers of romantic antebellum fictions penned novels dedicated to the preservation of the domestic sphere from the intrusion of politics or blacks who shared "social equality" with whites, by the late nineteenth and early twentieth centuries, both fictional and nonfictional writers had contributed to a vast catalog of titles devoted to white supremacy. From Thomas Dixon's *The Clansmen* (1905), on which D. W. Griffith based his 1915 film *Birth of a Nation*, to Margaret Mitchell's *Gone with the Wind* (1936), fictional writing popularized white supremacy and antiblack racism in an even broader way than popular nonfictional works that provided a "scientific" credibility for broadly held prejudices.

Antiblack racism featured prominently in nineteenth- and twentieth-century fiction and popular nonfiction writing. It is important to note, however, that white authors of fiction and nonfiction also drew on pseudoscientific theories of race to incorporate other ethno-racial groups into their narratives. Ideas about Native Americans being either a noble savage or a doomed race; Latinos constituted as lazy, "mongrelized" race; conniving Asians; or cliquish Jews and Eastern Europeans all appeared in the fiction and nonfiction literature that Americans consumed during the nineteenth and twentieth centuries.

American popular literature therefore reflected the racial prejudices of the vast majority of the American public. For example, perceptions of Native Americans as noble savages living in perfect harmony with nature had a long cultural tradition dating back to the sixteenth century. In North America, Rousseau's *A Discourse on the Origin of Inequality* (1755) and his discussion of "savage man" with "passions so little active, and so good a curb, men, being rather wild than wicked," merely acted in self-defense, guarding "themselves against the mischief that might be done them, than to do mischief to others," provided something of a cultural springboard from which generation after generation of American writers conceptualized Native Americans as noble savages.[45] For example, Julia Kemble Hatton's *Tammany, A Serious Opera* (1794) reworked Rousseau's formulation to characterize indigenous people as "ennobled savages" who were loyal, self-sacrificing individuals.[46]

By the early nineteenth century, the literary tradition of portraying Native Americans as noble savages had become commonplace in popular culture. In poetry, drama, short stories, novels, and nonfiction, the image of the noble savage was ubiquitous in American literary cultures. Most famously, the transcendental writers James Fenimore Cooper and Henry David Thoreau wrote of Native Americans in sentimental terms, marveling at the "indwelling" and intuitive spirituality that they perceived in indigenous people. These racialized perceptions received some of their clearest expressions in Henry Wadsworth Longfellow's epic poem *The Song of Hiawatha* (1855), in which Native Americans possess spiritual and emotional qualities that enable them to harness their instincts and live in harmony with "nature."[47]

Ralph Waldo Emerson wrote similarly in 1857, marveling at the ability of Native Americans to seemingly live in harmony with nature while also lamenting what he saw as the excesses of "civilized" and "industrialized" American society. Praising the "primitivism" that he imagined dwelt within Native Americans, Emerson expressed a profound regret for what he saw as the passing of the Native American from the world's stage, as they slid toward inevitable extinction in the face of expansive industrial civilizations. All the more reason, Thoreau felt, for white men to comprehend the Native American's knowledge of the natural world, a knowledge that civilized men had lost.[48] "An Indian has his knowledge for use," Emerson wrote approvingly, "and it only appears in use. Most white men that we know have theirs for talking purposes."[49]

Emerson's lament for the demise of Native Americans articulated a widely held racial belief in mid-nineteenth-century America that indigenous people were a doomed race. This idea coincided with the articulation of the United States' "manifest destiny" to extend the territorial limits of the republic from the Atlantic to the Pacific Oceans. Like "native" and "tribal" people in other colonial frontier societies—such as Canada, Australia, and New Zealand—white Americans too willingly accepted their own self-deception in proclaiming Native Americans a doomed people.[50]

The proslavery ideologue and popularizer of phrenology, Josiah Nott, spoke for many white Americans when he declared Native Americans to be a race of "untamable, carnivorous animals, which is fading away before civilization."[51] And those Native Americans who did survive the unceasing expansion of the Anglo-American civilization were not considered by Americans like Nott to be "real Indians," but "half-breeds" of questionable racial provenance.[52]

The themes of extinction, "mongrelization," and savagery proved ideal framing devices for American writers to express not only their racial perceptions of Native Americans but Mexicans and Mexican Americans throughout the southwestern borderlands. The representation of Mexican Americans also relied on pseudoscientific viewpoints to lend authoritativeness to Anglo-American perceptions of them as a degenerate, mongrelized wreckage of humanity because of Latin America's long history of intermarriage. Like other mixed-race people, Mexican Americans were routinely portrayed as being prone to mental illness and lacking in basic morals, qualities that made them prone to violence and crime. Vanderbilt University economics professor, Roy L. Garis, articulated such views as late as 1930. Garis, who viewed Mexican American people as "human swine," attempted to blame the Great Depression on Mexican Americans, writing of Mexican-origin people:

> [their] minds run to nothing higher than animal functions—eat, sleep, and sexual debauchery. In every huddle of Mexican shacks one meets the same idleness, hordes of hungry dogs, and filthy children with faces plastered with flies, disease, lice, human filth, stench, promiscuous fornication, bastardy, lounging, apathetic peons and lazy squaws, beans and dried chili, liquor, general squalor, and envy and hatred of the gringo. These people sleep by day and prowl by night like coyotes, stealing anything they can get their hands on, no matter how useless to them it may be. Nothing left outside is safe unless padlocked and chained down. Yet there are Americans clamoring for more of this human swine to be brought over from Mexico.[53]

Garis here articulated some of the most widely held racist beliefs about Mexican American people during the early twentieth century. Seemingly incapable of "civilized" standards of behavior, such people, Garis insisted, existed as the savage animals of the forest existed: they lived for the moment, acting on impulse rather than forethought. Moreover, Garis viewed Mexican American people as cliquish and dangerous to American society, preying on honest Americans as the coyote prowls for its prey under the cover of darkness. Believing Mexican-origin people unable or unwilling, or perhaps both to conform to American standards of "civilization," Garis expressed no sympathy for Mexican American people and would no doubt have applauded when states such as California began repatriating people of Mexican descent to Mexico during the Great Depression.[54]

Views of this nature found reinforcement in fictional writing. While Mexican-origin people made relatively few appearances in popular fiction during the late nineteenth and early twentieth centuries, when they did they appeared as racially stereotypical characters. At the time of the Mexican American War (1846–1848), a flurry of novels tapped into popular prejudices and contributed to the solidification of negative images of Mexican people. For example, George Lippard's 1847 pulp novel *Legends of Mexico* drew inspiration from anti-Mexican sentiment in the United States. A friend and confidant of fellow writer Edgar Allan Poe, Lippard was in many respects ahead of his times. He was a pro-union organizer and champion of the working class. However, like so many white Americans who were part of the union movement in the nineteenth and early twentieth centuries, Lippard also harbored viciously racist views about people of color, especially Native Americans and Mexicans. Lippard saw such groups as obstacles to the territorial expansion of the American republic. In *Legends of Mexico*, then, Lippard vented his spleen on such matters. The result was a jingoistic novel that echoed the nationalist fervor for the United States' manifest destiny, and in which Mexicans existed for two reasons: first, as the enemy of U.S. interests in the Western Hemisphere, and second, to represent a disappearing breed of mongrel savages. Lippard elaborated on these points, writing that "as the Aztec people, crumbled before the Spaniard, so will the mongrel race, moulded [*sic*] of Indian and Spanish blood, melt into, and be ruled by, the Iron Race of the North.... You cannot deny it.... God speaks it." He further referred to Mexicans as "a semi-barbarous horde of slaves."[55] Like many U.S.-Mexico war novels, Lippard blended historical events into his fictional narrative, thus weaving together a story about Mexican duplicity, savagery, and racial inferiority that demonstrated the superiority of "the new race from the north."[56]

Such sentiments continued after the war. The Cherokee writer John Rollin Ridge, for instance, penned a famous account of Joaquin Murrieta, *The Life and Adventures of Joaquín Murrieta: The Celebrated California Bandit*, an account subsequently plagiarized by other writers.[57] Part of the inspiration behind Zorro, in Ridge's telling Murrieta, was a bloodthirsty border bandit who wantonly murdered just about any white person crossing his path.

Ridge based his novel on many of the popular accounts and newspaper articles of Murrieta and used Murrieta to voice his own displeasure at the decades of injustices visited on the Cherokee people by the U.S. government.
His blending of contemporary journalistic accounts and his own fictional
narration gave the book a historical tenor; in fact, many who read it believed
it was an accurate description of Murrieta's exploits. What Ridge really created was a caricature of the man based on stereotypical representations of
Mexicans that ultimately gained the attention of a wider readership through
the Mexican bandit character in popular novels. One of the more famous
examples of this genre of fiction was O. Henry's *Cisco Kid*, a collection of
stories that also reinforced popular perceptions about Mexicans as lazy, violent, and untrustworthy.[58]

Many of the fictional works that focused on Mexicans and Mexican
Americans were geographically situated in the southwestern border region
of the United States. As such, border fiction emerged as a genre unto itself. It
reflected the discomfort of Americans with the seemingly porous nature of
the U.S. southernmost borders, just as it highlighted Mexican duplicity and
lawlessness, especially after 1910 and the onset of the Mexican Revolution.
Take, for instance, Will Comfort's 1925 novel *Somewhere South in Sonora*.[59]
Comfort's novel explored several prominent characters, including Mexican
bandits, prostitutes, and a mixed-race character Comfort described as half
Mexican, half American. Comfort has one of the characters of the novel
speak for many Americans when he states, "we used to call 'em greasers and
shoot 'em up a lot, not thinking much about it."[60]

Into the middle decades of the twentieth century, racial stereotypes
continued to define the way people of Mexican ancestry were portrayed
in American fiction. For example, in her 1952 novel *Giant*, Edna Ferber
introduced readers to a number of clichéd Mexican-origin characters.
The novel's convoluted plot revolved around Jordan "Bick" Benedict, who
left his Texas ranch, Reata, to buy a horse only to fall in love and marry
a woman named Leslie. Upon their return to Texas, Leslie is thrust into a
tense world involving Bick's sister, Luz, and her hired hand Jett Rink. Luz
is eventually killed, Jett inheriting her land, upon which he soon discovers
oil. That discovery culminates in interfamily rivalry that goes on for several
generations. The Mexican American characters in the story are mainly a
backdrop, appearing infrequently and rarely explored with any depth or
attention to detail. Most are simply depicted as farmhands. For instance, Jett
explained how the Benedicts acquired their land: "Bought it—hell! Took
it off a ignorant bunch of Mexicans didn't have the brains or guts to hang

onto it. Lawyers come in and finagled around and lawsuits lasted a hundred years and by the time they got through the Americans had the land and the greasers was out on their ears."[61] While a stereotypical depiction, complete with Mexicans described as "greasers," Jett's description was, nevertheless, accurate and an indication of how American fiction was starting to come to terms with the country's violent colonial past.

When Ferber's novel was brought to the movie screen, it was only the character of Juana, the wife of one of Bick's sons, who made a sustained appearance, usually as a foil who gets discriminated against, once at a hair salon and another time at a restaurant. That provided Leslie with the chance to show her anti-discriminatory side and intervene on Juana's behalf. Like many popular works, people of color thus appear as the victims of racism, but the heroes who battle against such persecution invariably appear as whites. Such was the case with Leslie. There was also the character of Angel Obregon III. He largely served as the resident pachuco, or Latino thug, in the novel; in the film he is transformed into a World War II soldier who is killed in action. The Mexican Americans depicted in the novel (and film) thus appear in stereotypical roles. When not acting as thugs, they appear as field hands, mothers, servants, or militant youths. Literary scholar Robert Leleux summarizes the significance of such portrayals when he observes that

> *Giant's* characters are eminently recognizable. The wildcatting Jett Rink is a ringer for Glenn McCarthy; the venerable Benedict clan bears more than a passing resemblance to the Briscoes; the Conquistador Hotel is Houston's glamorous old Shamrock Hilton; and Reata Ranch is the fabled King Ranch. At the time of *Giant's* publication, many reviewers suggested that Ferber's exaggerated choice of fictional subjects had resulted in a boorish, overblown book. But looking back on it now, I think she did a fairly commendable job of conveying the truth and spirit of our state.[62]

If racial stereotypes punctuated fictional accounts of Mexican and Mexican American people during the nineteenth and early twentieth centuries, racial caricatures also defined the roles of people of Asian descent in popular novels and nonfiction. This large body of writing drew considerable inspiration from contemporary events, most notably the political and cultural debates about immigration. Along the West Coast of the United States, Americans incorporated a variety of arguments—ranging from the sociological belief that Chinese immigrants created "opium dens" in American cities to pseudoscientific ideas about Asian migrants bringing contagious diseases in to the United States—to push the U.S. Congress for tighter immigration laws. Buoyed by the support of anti-immigrant groups, eugenicists who sowed fears about the "yellow peril" and the "rising tide of color," as well as the findings of the 1907 Dillingham Commission on immigration, tighter federal prohibitions on all Asian immigration (except Filipinos) in 1917 and subsequent immigration acts placed quotas on immigrants from specific parts of the world (especially eastern and southern Europe) in 1921 and again in 1924.[63]

Sax Rohmer's *Fu Manchu* novels tapped into American fears about the impact of immigration and widespread anti-Asian prejudices. Rohmer's first novel, *The Mysterious Dr. Fu-Manchu* (1913), which was purposefully retitled for Americans as *The Insidious Dr. Fu-Manchu* to establish the protagonist's sinister nature, described a fictional character based on all of the negative stereotypes about Asian men. The protagonist in Rohmer's novels, Dr. Fu Manchu, conformed to stereotypes about the mysterious, conniving, and ultimately sinister nature of Chinese characters in American popular culture. Rohmer's novels were subsequently made into motion pictures, as we detail in Chapter 2, but it was Sax Rohmer's novels that caught the reading public's attention and reinforced suspicions about just how serious the yellow peril was in the United States.[64]

Americans were first introduced to Rohmer's Dr. Fu Manchu in his 1913 novel *The Insidious Dr. Fu-Manchu*. The subtitle of Rohmer's novel provided readers with an initial clue about how the author conceived of Dr. Fu: *The Insidious Dr. Fu-Manchu, Being a Somewhat Detailed Account of the Amazing Adventures of Nayland Smith in His Trailing the Sinister Chinaman*. As we detailed in the Introduction, one of the principal stereotypical renderings of Asians, especially the Chinese, was as "Chinamen" and as "sinister" or "wily." Rohmer's subtitle therefore presaged the type of character readers would encounter when they began reading the novel, but fixed attention on the white hero of the story, Nayland Smith. Indeed, the duplicity, cunning, and tendency toward criminal behavior associated with Chinese men during the early twentieth century were juxtaposed against the way Rohmer introduced readers to Dr. Fu's nemesis, and the good guy in the story, Smith, who, with the assistance of his accomplice Dr. Petrie, works doggedly to investigate and bring Fu to justice.

The Insidious Dr. Fu-Manchu opens with Smith conversing with Dr. Petrie about a newly discovered criminal in London. That criminal is allegedly a master of poison and potion making, able to craft particular types of poisons for specific murders. Smith referred to this shadowy figure as a "perverted genius" and "a fiend who, unless my calculations are at fault, is now living in London and who regularly wars with pleasant weapons."[65] Rohmer subsequently reinforces the evil cunning of Fu Manchu when he has Smith exclaim:

> Imagine a person, tall, lean and feline, high-shouldered, with a brow like Shakespeare and a face like Satan, a close-shaven skull, and long, magnetic eyes of the true cat-green. Invest him with all the cruel cunning of an entire Eastern race, accumulated in one giant intellect, with all the resources of science past and present, with all the resources, if you will, of a wealthy government—which, however, already has denied all knowledge of his existence. Imagine that awful being, and you have a mental picture of Dr. Fu-Manchu, the yellow peril incarnate in one man.[66]

Although the story is set in London, American readers would have immediately recognized that what Rohmer described was the American fear of the yellow peril. The sinister figure whom Smith and Petrie pursued was a predatory creature who combined the qualities of a wild animal and the evil spirit of the devil. Such a character threatened Western "civilization" with destruction.

Rohmer explained to readers that Smith had been tracking the evil Dr. Fu for some time. Evidently Fu Manchu had murdered a series of men across Asia and had now arrived in England to carry out some mysterious plot. That plot involved a secret group of Far East leaders who aspired to topple the Western world so that Asia could dominate global affairs. What Dr. Fu was after, then, was the destruction of the white race. Smith leads efforts to prevent this destruction but finds that he's foiled at almost every turn. He even temporarily succumbs to one of Dr. Fu's madness serums. Not all was lost with Smith's eminent demise, however. Dr. Petrie subsequently took up the pursuit of Dr. Fu and eventually captured him and demanded that he restore Smith. Dr. Fu complied with Petrie's request, only to seemingly die in a fire. But this was not the end of Dr. Fu, as his death proved little more than a ruse that played out in a dozen more Rohmer *Fu Manchu* novels, just as in many other *Fu Manchu* books by other authors, and scores of motion pictures.

The racism embedded in Rohmer's fiction reappeared in other Rohmer *Fu Manchu* stories. The doctor and Chinese people more generally appear in these novels as evil, fiendish, and untrustworthy characters. They crowd together in opium dens and urban slums plotting against white people. But the message was also broader than that. As Petrie observed when capturing

Fu Manchu, had Dr. Fu succeeded it would have meant "the victory of the yellow races over the white."[67] As such, the *Fu Manchu* stories relate a tale about one civilization engaged in constant battle with another, of one race endeavoring to destroy another, and an irrational fear that white people could very well lose that battle.

In contrast to the Fu Manchu character, the detective Charlie Chan represented a different kind of Asian stereotype. Detective Chan was the brainchild of author Earl Derr Biggers. In his 1925 novel *The House without a Key*, Biggers introduced readers to Charlie Chan for the first time. Biggers based his novels on the Honolulu detective Chang Apana, whom he read about while vacationing in Hawaii. While Biggers described Chan in a variety of ways in his novels, often attempting to move away from yellow peril stereotypes, his descriptions of Chan were almost universally negative and highly racialized. For example, Biggers characterized Chan as fat, feminine, aping of white people, and assimilationist. Charlie Chan represented a yellow Uncle Tom, a Chinese character different from Fu Manchu perhaps, but one still displaying stereotypical attributes.[68]

Our discussion thus far has focused on prominent historical examples of fictional and nonfictional books that articulated popularly held racial beliefs and/or prejudices in American society during the nineteenth and first half of the twentieth centuries. We do not want to give the impression, however, that it was only adult readers who were exposed to such racist tropes. Children constituted a key demographic for publishers, just as children's literature played an important educational role in acculturating American children to the social and cultural expectations that came with racial belief systems.

Children's books played a powerful cultural role in American society because they taught children at a very young age how they should think about nonwhite people. Works such as Frank J. Green's counting rhyme *Ten Little Niggers* (1864), which first appeared in England and debuted in the United States as *Simple Addition by a Little Nigger* (1874); Mary Wade's *Ten Little Indians* (1904); or the *Tintin* stories were published in Europe and sold in the United States.[69] Other works, such as Mark Twain's *The Adventures of Huckleberry Finn* (1884), while a classic and considered by many literary scholars to be antiracist, used the word "nigger" over 200 times and featured the character Jim, a runaway slave who comes across as simple and is frequently made the butt of jokes.[70] Laura Ingalls Wilder in the *Little House* stories also echoed popular racial tropes, especially about native peoples. In a number of chapters focusing on Native Americans, Wilder described Native Americans as "wild," "savages," "fierce and terrible," and having eyes "like snake's eyes."[71]

Perhaps the most famously racist, and very popular, children's story was Walt Disney's *Mickey Mouse and the Boy Thursday* (1948). Disney's Mickey Mouse was already a household name when *Mickey Mouse and the Boy Thursday* arrived in bookstores. The book began with Mickey discovering a black, tribal-looking character in a box of "west African bananas." This character, as Mickey describes him, had a "funny brown face" with "big black eyes." The book's illustrations enhance the narrative, providing children with a drawing of a blackface individual with white lips, his hair tied up on top of his head (but no bone), with an animal tooth necklace, and wearing a loin cloth. When Mickey asks his name, he replies "glug-ga-booch," which later in the story morphs into "booch-ga-blug." Mickey exclaims that the black boy looks like a man he used to know named Friday. The black boy shows Mickey a note from Friday affixed to his back explaining that this is Friday's "almost twin brother name Thursday." "I sendum to you," Friday explains in dialect, "for edumcation cause he needum background polished."

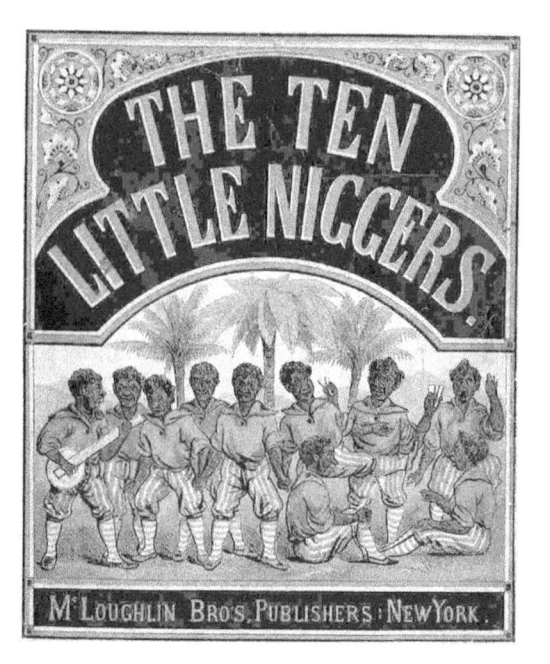

Part of what made the publishing industry so racist was its marketing to children. Here, children are taught basic arithmetic via the counting rhyme "Ten Little Niggers."

This stereotypical introduction provides Mickey with a segue to embark on a series of mishap-filled adventures with Thursday. These adventures give Mickey an opportunity to civilize Thursday. For example, Thursday tries to eat Mickey's goldfish and flowers, so Mickey redirects his friend by serving him a large meal, which Thursday devours. To amplify the uncivilized eating habits of Thursday, Disney has him eat the dishes also. Similar hijinks ensue when Mickey tries to bathe Thursday, with his protégé drinking all of the bath water. "He doesn't know any better," Mickey says to himself (and explains to the reader), "I'll just have to be patient and teach him the right way to do things." However, Thursday has a difficult time mastering Mickey's lessons. He throws a spear at the radio, attacks Minnie Mouse (who calls him a "beast" and "a savage"), and tries to roast a picture of a fish. Thursday ultimately meets Goofy and thinks he's some sort of deity. More mayhem ensues. Finally Thursday returns home and Mickey figures out that he thought Goofy was a living totem pole. "Well, thus dim-witted little monkey!" Goofy exclaims, "I allus said he didn't have no sense!"

Mickey Mouse and the Boy Thursday tapped into racial stereotypes that millions of white Americans had of African-descent people in the mid-twentieth century. For instance, although he looks more like a fully grown adult, Thursday is called a "boy" throughout the story, a term used during Jim Crow segregation to demean African American men. Much of the story, though, focuses on Thursday's overeating. This may have been a passive reference to stereotypes about black people mooching off hardworking Americans or a general reference to white perceptions about black gluttony, but this emphasis sought to convey a deeper meaning. Thursday, the moral of the story instructs children, represents such a backward, uneducated tribal African that he is foolish enough to think Goofy is an idol. To reinforce Thursday's savagery and simplicity of his intellect, the various characters in the book consistently refer to him as a "savage" and a "little monkey," all pejorative terms used to denigrate black people in Jim Crow America.[72]

Conclusion

Learning the social etiquette of race relations in nineteenth- and twentieth-century America meant internalizing the lessons gleaned from books. Whether works of popular fiction or nonfiction that appealed to antiblack prejudices, anti-immigrant sentiment against Asian and Mexican people, or racism against Native Americans, the printed word played a significant cultural role in normalizing racism in American society. Novels, as literary scholar Ann Folwell Stanford reminds us, are about "seeing" the world in which we live. And the world of nineteenth- and twentieth-century America was a world seen through the lens of race and racism.[73]

Fictional and nonfictional works are also important because they allowed readers to create images in their heads based on their broader understanding of the world. Authors certainly make worlds, but more often than not they describe people and concepts and places in ways that readers already understand, or at least they think they understand. The writers of the nineteenth and twentieth centuries often spoke to people's pre-held beliefs, while they worked to create other realties, either in fiction or in nonfiction, that helped to also confirm people's preconceived notions of the racialized world around them. Pseudoscientific race thinkers, for instance, created a host of overly contrived accounts. Many of these scholars (and we use that term lightly), however, already believed nonwhites to be inferior to whites, and so they concocted a variety of scientific reports that verified their beliefs. Many of their beliefs, moreover, were already largely accepted by millions of Americans and, as such, these authors developed fictitious scientific studies that confirmed what many people already thought and believed.

But nineteenth- and twentieth-century Americans saw the world through more than just the printed word. They saw it reproduced in theater, in song, and in oral narratives. These genres of media ran the gamut from highbrow to lowbrow humor. As we discuss in Chapter 2, few mediums proved as effective in packaging the racial messages of these various story-telling outlets than popular advertisements. As our analysis reveals, advertisements and marketing campaigns, combined with movies and television, provided an ideal cultural format to expand on the racist ideas that had been developing in fiction and nonfiction writing during the nineteenth and twentieth centuries. In the process, American advertising reified racist stereotypes and facilitated what two scholars recently labeled as the "communication of hate."[74]

Chapter 2

Marketing Discrimination

In early 1888, business entrepreneurs Charles Underwood and Christopher Rutt purchased a defunct flour mill in rural Missouri. They hoped to expand operations, but soon found themselves in a glutted market with surplus flour filling a small warehouse. The two men needed to find a way to market this flour, and so they began mixing batches of ready-to-make pancake mix. Their ready-to-make formula, offered in an unassuming white paper bag, sold poorly, that is until Rutt stumbled upon a marketing strategy designed to appeal to his largely local and southern clientele. At a minstrel show in 1889, Rutt witnessed a performance by a white male actor in blackface and drag who impersonated a black female figure called "Aunt Jemima." Rutt realized instantly that this Aunt Jemima, the southern Mammy incarnate, not only represented culinary expertise but could symbolize a product so easy to make that it was almost as if your black servant had done it for you. Thus Aunt Jemima the pancake queen was born, a figure whose name graces countless products today and is a multimillion-dollar industry, but one rooted in the advertising industry's racist history.[1]

The advertising industry is an old one and exists to serve clients who want to market and sell products. The industry, however, does more than this; it both mirrors and creates images of life that people (or consumers) internalize and ultimately define as normative.[2] The historian Jackson Lears contends that advertising has played an important role in American society in promoting a "certain vision of the good life" that is acquired through the purchase of goods. According to this view, advertising aims to appeal to human desires and wants, and so plays on our inner fantasies.[3] Advertising also fosters a sense of "imagined community" and nurtures a psychology of "peer pressure" to promote consensus around a broad range of social and cultural issues.[4] In other words, advertising and marketing creates, as Lears puts it, a "symbolic universe where certain cultural values were sanctioned and others rendered marginal or invisible."[5]

The advertising industry's use of race and racist imagery provides us with an instructive example of how mass media institutions contribute to the shaping of social and cultural norms. Professional advertising and marketing firms emerged in the United States and other parts of the Western world during the latter third of the nineteenth century. In Britain, for example, late nineteenth-century advertisers played a crucial role in providing white Britons with a racial language that became central to articulating a sense of superiority in the British Empire. Anne McClintock refers to this as "commodity racism." McClintock's defines "commodity racism" as the idea that certain consumer goods acquired fixed racial and cultural meanings. For example, Pears' soap developed a marketing campaign that played on popular associations of racial identity and personal hygiene. Pears' soap was thus portrayed as an instrument of British civilization, capable of "brightening the dark corners of the earth."[6]

In the United States, a similar cultural process was under way during the late nineteenth century. Historian Kristin Hoganson refers to this process as "cosmopolitan domesticity." Hoganson argues that at the turn of the nineteenth and twentieth centuries, a growing number of daily and weekly publications, expanding trade markets, and increasing income levels, enabled white Americans to let more of the outside world into their homes without Americans having to leave their homes. With rising income levels, an increasingly bourgeois consumer population purchased literature, "Turkish curtains," "Oriental" rugs, and "knickknacks from around the globe," which entered into the dining rooms and parlors of white Americans without disrupting the racial tranquility of their homes.[7] The incorporation of these items into American homes did not require a commitment to, or belief in, equality among human beings. Rather, in an era when many millions of white Americans shared a common set of racial stereotypes about African Americans and Native Americans and felt unsettled by the "influx" of immigrations from Southeast Asia, Latin America, and southern and eastern Europe, cosmopolitan domesticity allowed white middle-class Americans to indulge in an "orientalist" aesthetic in which the "otherness" of non-white people reinforced, rather than challenged, their sense of racial superiority.[8]

In appealing to such sensibilities, American advertisers had a ready means with which to make money while at the same time reinforcing commonly held racial beliefs among most white Americans. This proved especially true when advertisers drew inspiration from racial imagery within the United States, such as blackface minstrelsy. The use of blackface characters such as Aunt Jemima in advertising campaigns highlights how "commodity racism" exploited racial stereotypes to market everything from jam, maple syrup, hair care products, and, most famously, instant pancake mix.[9] Moreover, the use of these stock racial depictions demonstrates one of the key ways in which racism became institutionalized in the American popular media. Like works of fiction and nonfiction, advertising became one of the most important ways by which the media communicated a racist vision to the American people during the twentieth century.

Images of African Americans and Native Americans in Advertising

The likeness of African American adults and children was used to advertise scores of products during the nineteenth and twentieth centuries. In all forms of media, American consumers saw, heard, and/or watched advertisements for products that featured "pickaninnies," "aunties," "uncles," and "Sambos," as well as more offensive terminology such as "nigger" or "darkie" to market a variety of products. Such images perpetuated racial ideologies of white supremacy in which blackness represented subservience and justified discrimination because it helped to define a world in which black people labored for the betterment of whites.[10]

The ideology of white supremacy had become so commonplace by the latter half of the nineteenth century that it seemed normal to white Americans that African Americans "naturally" occupied a subordinate status in American society. The nascent advertising industry was not shy about exploiting such beliefs. For example, the marketing of late nineteenth-century consumer novelties drew inspiration from the racial slapstick of minstrel shows and their use of comic characters—such as the "jolly nigger"—or the grinning, watermelon-eating "pickaninny." In other instances, American carnivals and circuses featured a dunking booth, often labeled "Dump the Nigger" or "Coon Dip." These games taught white children to take pleasure in harming a black target. It also taught boys and girls that violence against a black target should not be taken too seriously and was in fact something to laugh about.[11]

Late nineteenth- and early twentieth-century advertisers presented childhood as a period of life filled with educational lessons. Embedded in these life lessons were constant reminders about African American inferiority. For instance, children learned the importance of thrift by saving their pennies in a Jolly Nigger Bank, a product patented by J. E. Stevens Company of Connecticut in 1892. Alternatively, children could play card games and solve puzzles that carried racist titles with their siblings, parents, and adult relatives between the 1870s and 1890s. In 1874, McLoughlin Brothers of New York released a jigsaw puzzle that was marketed with the title "Chopped Up Niggers." Not to be outdone, Parker Brothers began selling a card game called "The Game of Ten Little Niggers" in 1895. A variation on the famous "Old Maid," "The Game of Ten Little Niggers" involved a deck of black characters, with one "oddball" character. The participant left with the oddball lost the game.[12]

The imagery of African and/or African American children also appeared in numerous advertising campaigns for personal hygiene products during the early twentieth century. Public awareness of human health and hygiene reached new heights during the period historians refer to as the Progressive Era. This was a period in American history in which political reformers addressed issues of urban poverty and disease, among many other things. It was also an era that intersected with the heyday of the eugenics movement, a loosely organized but racially charged collection of scholars, politicians, and social activists who worried that Anglo-Americans were being "swamped" by immigrant populations from outside Western Europe and that the "colored" populations of the world were reproducing themselves at a much faster rate than the world's "white races."[13]

As Americans awoke to the personal health benefits of regular bathing, advertisers played a pivotal role in promoting personal hygiene products. They did this, not surprisingly, by exploiting the racist and xenophobic anxieties of white Americans. One of the more prominent advertising campaigns of the early twentieth century featured the "The Gold Dust Twins." The advertisements portrayed two semi-naked African boys promoting Fairbank's Gold Dust Soap. The Gold Dust twins drew on popular events, in this case the aeronautical accomplishments of the Wright brothers. In a play on words, the advertisers use the punchline: "The Right Brothers to Make the Dirt Fly."[14] The twins are stereotypically dark black pickaninnies with bright red lips, one of the most common ways advertisers portrayed black people at this time.

The Gold Dust Twins campaign was the brainchild of G.H.E. Hawkins, a Chicago-based advertiser. Hawkins said of the Gold Dust Twins campaign that "the poster is our best outdoor advertisement, and, to my mind, the biggest hit that has ever been made in posting."[15] Indeed, just as Pears' soap became a leading brand name in the United Kingdom using advertisements that portrayed exotic, racialized "others," so Hawkins capitalized on a similar racial imagery in the United States to successfully promote Gold Dust

Soap. The Gold Dust Twins marketing campaign attempted to capitalize on racist imagery without using racist terminology. Other advertisers were not so kind. Chlorinol bleach soap, for example, promoted its product with an ad featuring a raft occupied by three African American children, two dark and one light skinned. The darker skinned children say, "We are going to use Chlorinol and be like de white nigger."[16]

As we have seen earlier, in many cases the use of racist terms helped sell products. As with the usage of racist terminology like "nigger" or "coon," advertisers often utilized language in their products. "Nigger Head Oysters" and "Nigger Head Stove Polish" serve as good examples. There was also the popular toy/souvenir "Darkey in a Watermelon," a papier mache watermelon with a pickaninny inside. "Darkie Brand" toothpaste, soap, and other personal hygiene products were primarily marketed in Asian nations and Australia, but numerous other products used the term "darkie" to sell similar products in the United States.

Perhaps the most effective ethno-racial term used in advertising was "Sambo." That word graced the exteriors of hundreds of different products in the late nineteenth and the early to mid-twentieth centuries. The products ranged from the obscure—"Sambo Axle Grease" and the "Dancing Sambo" party puppet—to the popular and easily recognizable—such as Sambo chocolate malted milk or "Sambo Brand" watermelons. Sambo chocolate milk and the Sambo Brand watermelons are good examples of how stereotypical imagery of black Americans helped sell products. Sambo Brand, for instance, featured a wide-grinning black man with vibrantly white teeth about to devour a slice of watermelon. The Sambo chocolate milk featured a blackface depiction of an African American man, complete with dark black burnt cork skin, ruby red lips, and white coloration around his eyes, dressed as a servant or bellhop. The ads encouraged people to "drink Sambo." Such advertisements were ubiquitous, appearing in countless storefronts, newspapers, or magazines.

Indeed, it was difficult to avoid racial imagery in American advertisement during the first half of the twentieth century. In an industry dominated by white men, racialized and sexist imagery became the norm. For example, Maxwell House advertised its coffee in the 1930s using male servers in blackface, who said things such as "golly, Mis' Maria, folks jus' can't help havin' a friendly feelin' for dis heah coffee." General Electric promoted its new range of kitchen sinks in the 1940s using a black domestic declaring "I'se sure got a good job <u>now!</u>" GE also promoted its range of electric ovens using the image of a young African American boy eating a piece of fried chicken, the caption reading "Um-m-m! Um-m-m! m-m-m! Yo next range should be a General Electric." Plymouth advertised many of its 1940s model cars with similar black servant–type ads.

One of the most profitable corporations to emerge during the twentieth century was Monsanto Chemicals. One of its most famous advertisements featured a plantation scene in which African American men and children pick cotton somewhere "below Mason and Dixon's line." The slogan attached to the image reads: "It's Plastics Picking Time down South."[17] Monsanto's use of this image focused on three smiling children as they frolicked in piles of cotton while their mother looks on and their father carries a heavy basket of cotton. The image drew on the nostalgia of the Lost Cause, portraying innocent, happy, and contented African Americans working and playing in the cotton fields. Implicit in this advertisement was the concept that the products produced by Monsanto Chemicals will prove as labor-saving as slavery did for white Americans—particularly white southerners—prior to the Civil War. Thus, Monsanto produced an advertisement well suited to markets in the American South, a region of the country where political and business leaders strove to continually increase the economic activity of the region.

While all of the these advertisements exploited racial stereotypes about Africans and/or African Americans, few marketing campaigns have proven to be as enduring as Aunt Jemima's Pancake and Waffle mixes. The literary scholar and journalist Diane Roberts writes that "Aunt Jemima is so familiar she is practically invisible."[18] Roberts's observation brings to the foreground a cultural phenomenon that often goes unnoticed by twenty-first-century consumers as they idle down supermarket aisles throughout the United States. Aunt Jemima, smiling as she did in the 1920s and seemingly frozen in time, has become part of our consumer landscape, an icon in American advertising. Her image on boxes of instant pancake mix hearkens back to the days of slavery; it is also an image that makes Quaker Oates—the owner of Aunt Jemima pancake mix—over $300 million annually.[19] As the company's website proudly declares, "For over a century, Aunt Jemima® Pancake & Waffle Mixes and Syrups have been a favorite with loving moms and dads who take pride in preparing hot, delicious breakfasts for their families."[20]

The Aunt Jemima brand owes its origins to blackface minstrelsy in nineteenth-century America. In the 1820s and 1830s, T. D. Rice's performances of "Jumpin' Jim Crow" on stages in the Bowery District of New York and elsewhere in the United States became hugely popular, especially among urban audiences. Rice's act, in which he appeared in blackface with raggedy clothing and performed an odd, contorted dance, enabled the performer to "cross over" and "become" something that he was not. His "Jumpin' Jim Crow" routine thus expanded on a Western cultural tradition of masquerades and carnivalesque revelry. However, when Rice and other blackface minstrel performers finished their routines and walked off the stage, they could wipe the burnt cork from their faces and resume lives as white Americans, with all of the socioeconomic advantages associated with such an identity. Such public displays of racial power proved largely unattainable to African Americans during the nineteenth and early twentieth centuries.[21]

Minstrelsy, however, was more than an outlet for white performers to express their white privilege. It was also an arena in which predominantly working-class Americans and recently arrived immigrants from Europe could learn and then nurture a sense of racial superiority over African Americans. Minstrelsy was therefore a form of working-class consumerism. It was also educational, teaching immigrants and Americans how to regard black people. Audiences paid for the privilege of seeing blackface performers entertain them in a way that made them laugh and cheer. They laughed, for example, at jokes that reinforced their sense of white privilege at the expense of feckless, bumbling "Negroes," and songs that repeated lines that defined what an "authentic Negro" looked and sounded like. In other words, the singing and joking, often delivered in dialect, created a sense of "authenticity," while the lyrics associated with the music of minstrelsy—"darkies," "niggers," and "jigaboos"—became embedded in American popular culture.[22]

Out of this cultural context, Aunt Jemima—the plump, smiling, apron-wearing mammy—emerged. In 1889, Chris Rutt, a Milwaukee native and managing editor of the St. Joseph News-Press, had attended a minstrel show and saw a performance of "Old Aunt Jemima," a popular nineteenth-century minstrel song. The performance inspired Rutt, who, with business partner Charles Underwood, sought a hook to attract consumers to their new brand of instant pancake and waffle mixes. In 1890, Rutt and Underwood's R. T. Davis Milling Company had their hook. They developed a marketing campaign and hired Nancy Green, an ex-slave from Kentucky, to portray Aunt Jemima in advertising their product. As Jim Crow segregation swept across the American South, an icon of American advertising emerged.

In 1926, Quaker Oats purchased R. T. Davis and developed the Aunt Jemima character. Over the course of the twentieth century, Aunt Jemima went through a number of minor changes to her image. However, these changes tended to be subtle rather than substantive. Over the decades, the asexual, chubby, loyal domestic represented in Aunt Jemima has remained. Aunt Jemima represented a safe and reassuring figure, a character (or caricature) from an imagined past that fit neatly with Lost Cause mythology and the fiction of the slave South as a happy, idyllic, prosperous place, in which kindly masters and nurturing mistresses oversaw the work of loyal and contented slaves. As one scholar observes, the "black cook/domestic, often referred to as Mammy, exists to do nothing but prepare and serve food" and to dispense a "hearty helping of homespun wisdom about life."[23]

In promoting a highly romanticized image of the slave South, Quaker Oats was able to blend historical nostalgia with the upwardly mobile aspirations of twentieth-century Americans. This proved particularly true for the growing white middle class. As American advertisers worked overtime to market a growing range of labor-saving technologies that promised to make life for the "average housewife" more "efficient," Quaker Oats exploited the image of Aunt Jemima with the promise, as one scholar observes, that a black woman "in the kitchen kept white women out of it."[24]

Such promises seemed a little more tangible when radio listeners were introduced to the Aunt Jemima Variety Hour in the early twentieth century. Listeners could tune in to Aunty Jemima, and her paternalistic white male counterpart, and hear stories that promised to bring "happiness" to every American household. Key to such happiness was a very specific type of historical nostalgia, a nostalgia in which Aunt Jemima's white male counterpart routinely asked for "One of your old plantation sayings, if you will." Aunt Jemima replied to such requests by declaring, "It's a pleasure folks to remind ya'll that the Lord meant for the sky to be blue, but if the day is blue it's probably our fault." Brightening one's day, at least in the world of the Aunt Jemima Variety Hour, required one to purchase the easy-to-prepare Aunt Jemima pancake and waffle mix.

By the 1930s and 1940s, the Aunt Jemima Variety Hour had made enormous strides in cementing the place of Aunt Jemima pancake and waffle mixes in American popular and consumer culture. A generation of radio listeners had now grown up with "smiling, happy, Aunt Jemima" offering them her "thought of the day." They had also learned that Aunt Jemima's pancake and waffle mix was as "easy as one-two-three" to prepare. Indeed, the image of the loyal and wise Mammy, with her "secret recipe," ensured that customers who purchased Aunt Jemima's pancake and waffle mixes were guaranteed "honest-to-goodness tentilatin' Old South flavor." What's more, Aunt Jemima declared in a classic rendition of "Negro dialect" that her pancakes were "Happifyin'" and "sho' sets folks singin'!" And just in case consumers did not learn about Aunt Jemima's promises from their radio sets, one need only glance at a box of Aunt Jemima's pancake and waffle mix to know that Aunt Jemima brought families together and made everyone happy because Aunt Jemima's pancake and waffle mixes were like "having another pair of hands in the house" that would enable mothers to prepare "a temptin' lunch chilluns love."[25]

By the 1950s, television changed advertising and saw the introduction of such programs as "Aunt Jemima presents Peggy and Chuck," a program about a white couple living in suburban America with their infant son. While still exploiting the nostalgic fiction propagated by Lost Cause mythologizers, such programs placed the aspirations of Americans within the context of Cold War culture. With the perceived threat of communism, the Soviet Union emerging as a perceived external threat to America's consumer culture, and a rising wave of civil rights protests challenging Jim Crow segregation from within, the advertising of Aunt Jemima's pancake and waffle mix—topped with Uncle Remus Syrup, "dis sho' am good!"—offered white Americans some reassuring images from a less complicated past. What could be simpler, after all, than "perfect pancakes in ten shakes."

Programs like "Aunt Jemima presents Peggy and Chuck" attempted to prescribe the American dream for Cold War Americans. This dream involved a vision of white suburban prosperity framed by images of happy black domestics loyally working to perpetuate the happiness of white households. Put simply, television in Cold War culture could be used as a tool that perpetuated assumptions about the racial hierarchy of American society. Similarly, television could reinforce patriarchal gender norms. In one episode of "Aunt Jemima presents Peggy and Chuck," a scene depicting Chuck in the kitchen with Aunt Jemima's pancake mix prompts Peggy to quip, "This is the kitchen not your workshop."

The intersecting, and often mutually reinforcing, categories of race and gender were hallmarks of Aunt Jemima television advertising during the 1950s and 1960s. Increasingly, however, Aunt Jemima appeared in television commercials only as an inanimate image on a box of pancake mix. White couples acted out scenes that served to prescribe middle-class ideals for television viewers. This proved the case with one of the most popular shows on American television, the *Ozzie and Harriet Show*, sponsored by Aunt Jemima's Pancake and Waffle mix. In one scene from the early 1960s, the Nelson family sits around their breakfast table as they enjoy Aunt Jemima pancakes. Herein lies another aspect of Aunt Jemima advertising during the 1960s: the promotion of family values. Strikingly, happiness, unity, and prosperity were portrayed as values that were attainable in suburbs occupied by predominantly white families, not in the increasingly black "ghettoes" in inner-city America.

Aunt Jemima was not the only "loyal" black figure used to reinforce images of white prosperity and suburban tranquility during the mid-twentieth century. Another icon of American advertising to emerge during the twentieth century was "Uncle Ben." The Uncle Ben character emerged as Aunt Jemima's male counterpart in the 1940s. He was the creation of Gordon L. Harwell and was based on the visage of restaurant maître d' Frank Brown. Together Harwell and Brown created the corporate logo for Uncle Ben's Converted Rice Company.

The Uncle Ben character played on stereotypes of the elderly, nonthreatening, black man in American culture. It also borrowed on imagery, not unlike Aunt Jemima, dating back to nineteenth-century minstrelsy. Despite this, executives from Uncle Ben's Converted Rice Company insisted that the inspiration for the corporate logo came from a rice farmer in Houston, Texas, whom locals referred to as Uncle Ben. Uncle Ben's last name is unknown. Revealingly, very little is known about the real-life Uncle Ben. For example, was he anyone's uncle, or was the use of that title consistent with the common southern tradition of referring to older black men as "uncle?" What is known is that Harwell apparently sketched Uncle Ben's likeness shortly before the elderly Houston rice farmer's death. From those drawings, Uncle Ben entered the pantheon of racialized advertising images in the United States.[26]

As was the case with Aunt Jemima, the Uncle Ben character was part of a general trend among American advertisers to use pickaninnies and black aunties and uncles in marketing campaigns.[27] Such titles demarcated the racial otherness of African Americans, but did so in nonthreatening ways. In fact, such characters had the potential to enhance the well-being of the white people they served. Uncle Ben's rice, for example, promised consumers that "its sunny color—like magic—cooks up white and fluffy." Uncle Ben's Converted Rice Company was so confident that customers would be satisfied with their product that each box of its rice came emblazoned with the promise of "Guaranteed fluffy, or your money back!"[28] Only in the early 2000s was Uncle Ben modified: he was shown in an opulent office and is supposed to be the CEO of the company.

While the preceding analysis makes clear the pervasive use of racist imagery in American advertising, both advertisers and entrepreneurs also recognized that African Americans were also consumers. Appealing to "Negro markets," however, was often not the top priority of America's business elites. Nowhere was the complex and often uneasy relationship between the advertising industry and the African American population more apparent during the twentieth century than in the competition between Coca-Cola and Pepsi.

The rise of Coca-Cola is the stuff of American legend. Virtually every American has some vague sense of the company's growth and global expansion during the twentieth century. Coca-Cola was the brainchild of Dr. John Pemberton, an Atlanta pharmacist, who developed Coca-Cola in 1886. Pemberton sold the rights to his formula to Asa Candler, who marketed Coke as a cure for headaches. A broader market beckoned, however, and after Coke's formula underwent modification, it began to be distributed to soda fountains during the 1910s. The Coca-Cola Company quickly developed national brand recognition following its purchase by Ernest Woodruff in 1919. In 1923, Woodruff's son, Robert W. Woodruff, a vocal opponent of "racial mixing," took control of Coca-Cola and transformed the company into the cultural icon that it is today.[29]

Coca-Cola began to recognize the potential value of appealing to the African American market only in the 1950s. James Farley, the export chairman at Coca-Cola, announced in 1955 that the "15 billion dollar Negro Market" constituted a "vast, unexploited market-within-a-market." Coca-Cola subsequently began running advertisements in African American publications such as *Ebony* and employed black personalities such as Floyd Patterson and Sugar Ray Robinson to spread the word that "There's nothing like Coke."[30] Not until the 1970s, however, did African Americans begin climbing up the corporate ladder at Coca-Cola.

Coca-Cola's major competitor, the Pepsi-Cola Company, recognized the untapped market potential among African American consumers long before executives at Coke awakened to the presence of this "unexploited market-within-a-market." Pepsi, invented by Caleb Bradham, a North Carolina "druggist," in 1898, was originally sold at drugstores as a tonic for "a tired soul." Pepsi's growth in popularity was rapid, with over 240 bottling franchises in the United States by 1910. By this time, advertisers marketed Pepsi as a "pure, food drink." Such claims were possible because the company did not have to remove any "dangerous ingredients" from its product after the federal government's Pure Food and Drug Act (1907) clamped down on the infusion of narcotic substances in products like soft drinks (Coke famously contained cocaine during its early years of production).

Indeed, the absence of substances such as caffeine in Pepsi led Bradham to devise an advertising program directed at children who would "grow up healthy" if they consumed Pepsi-Cola.[31]

It was the African American market that Pepsi was truly able to capitalize on. At the end of World War II, Coke dominated the American soft-drink market. Americans associated Coca-Cola with Santa Claus and the American G.I., engendering a strong brand loyalty among consumers. Pepsi therefore had its work cut out for it if it hoped to erode at least some of Coke's market share. Pepsi's challenge was a difficult one. At the end of the war, the company was in the process of trying to claw its way out of several decades of turbulence, numerous bankruptcies, and multiple changes in ownership. Under the leadership of Walter S. Mack from 1938 to 1950, Pepsi actively began marketing to black consumers. These early campaigns proved to be so successful that by the time Mack left Pepsi in 1950, Pepsi-Cola was known colloquially as "nigger Coke."[32]

On the brink of bankruptcy again in 1950, a new advertising campaign—centered on the slogan of "Pepsi-Cola, The Light Refreshment" and "Pepsi-Cola hits the spot"—helped to turn the company around. The white corporate leaders at Pepsi targeted the black market in the early twentieth century with a barrage of advertising campaigns that ran into the many millions of dollars. Edward F. Boyd, who joined Pepsi-Cola in 1947, was placed in charge of developing an advertising campaign for the Negro market. Boyd oversaw the training of a sales team that included African American sales and marketing staff. Boyd also provided staff with "diversity training" to help his sales and marketing teams forge brand loyalty among African American consumers.

As early as the 1930s and 1940s, Pepsi began promoting its product in African American publications. Like Chevrolet, Lever Brothers, Esso Standard Oil, and tobacco giant Lucky Strike—whose advertising slogan was "First in Negro History … First in Cigarettes"—Pepsi advertisements appeared in black newspapers and weeklies. At the same time, Pepsi's African American sales and market representatives ("Brown Hucksters" in a 1948 *Ebony* article) promoted its product at Duke Ellington concerts, provided sponsorships to African American high schools and colleges, and peddled Pepsi in black communities.[33] By the early 1950s, these campaigns were so successful that the vast majority of African American soft-drink consumers were three times more likely to purchase Pepsi over Coke.[34]

Coca-Cola and Pepsi demonstrate the double-edged sword that is advertising mixed with race. On the one hand, African Americans were the perfect foils for American advertisers: easy to mock, fun to laugh at, and their images helped sell products. On the other hand, as Pepsi wisely discovered, African Americans constituted an untapped market that could work to the benefit of corporations. While Pepsi may have been ridiculed as "nigger Coke," it successfully attracted black consumers in a way that Coke did not.

The prominence of caricatured images of African American in late nineteenth- and twentieth-century advertisements reflected the pervasiveness of the black–white racial binary in American culture and the impact of nostalgic images of slavery and the Old South. There existed few industries that did not try to exploit such imagery in their advertising. In 1934, for example, like the cola companies, Anheuser-Busch promoted its Budweiser beer by using stock racial depictions. In one ad, the image of a stately older white gentleman is served by a dark-skinned African American waiter. The caption reads: "Good times coming, Boss."

Racial representations also dominated tobacco advertising during the late nineteenth and early twentieth centuries. These representations ranged from the crude, such as the Milwaukee-based B. Leidersdory Company that produced "Nigger Hair Smoking tobacco" or "Nigger Boy Licorice Cigarettes" (which featured a large smiling pickaninny, their tagline reading: "of all the sweets, so full of joy, the best of all, is Nigger Boy"), to the standard racist depictions of ethnic others. The tobacco industry did not rely solely on racial stereotypes of African Americans to advertise its products. Images of exotic locations and non-Caucasian peoples routinely advertised tobacco products. In the early twentieth century, Abdullah's cigarettes ran advertisements for its "Virginia no. 7," "Turkish no. 11," and "Egyptian no. 16" products. The advertisements, which appeared in popular periodicals and billboards, featured exotic scenes of seduction, riches, and colonial excess. Such advertisements represented a commercial form of orientalism in which images of colonized others in the Middle East, North Africa, Asia, and to a lesser extent to a by-gone era in North America promised a pleasurable, decadent experience.[35]

As in other advertisements of this era, the mocking of black Americans helped sell cigarettes. Bull Durham, for instance, introduced a popular magazine advertising blitz in the late 1890s and early 1900s that prominently featured common blackface caricatures of African Americans. In an ad from 1900, for example, two big, red-lipped, and dark black men, as well as a pickaninny child, all of whom wore shoddy, mismatched clothing, have been out hunting. Having no way to light their cigarettes, they use their rifles. The caption of the ad reads: "without a match." In another ad from 1900, the company depicted a bucolic country scene with a mammy and two pickaninnies seated in front of a country store. One of the pickaninnies, a young girl with bright red lips and nappy hair tied in bows, salivates over a large slice of watermelon. The Mammy figure enjoys a smoke. The caption for the ad is a black vernacular statement: "My! It shure am Sweet Tastan."

By far the most commonly used images in tobacco advertising centered on Native Americans. Tobacco companies used Native American imagery to market tobacco products such as "the Red Man's gift." Advertising agencies were also not shy in promoting the health benefits of cigarettes by using visual and textual allusions to "Indian medicine men" and the medicinal properties of smoking tobacco.[36] Indeed, the links among tobacco manufacturers, the advertising industry, and major American universities were often used to reinforce the message of tobacco's medicinal benefits. In Richmond, Virginia, the Medical Center of Virginia (MCV), the medical school of Virginia Commonwealth University, forged close ties with tobacco giants such as Philip Morris and the American Tobacco Company. From as early as the 1940s, a revolving door of university officials and tobacco industry insiders ensured a particularly close relationship between big tobacco and medical research at institutions like MCV. As historian Robert Proctor observes, for "nearly three quarters of a century, VCU has been the tobacco industry's most important academic ally and collaborator."[37]

The type of support from major research institutions that Proctor describes in his research helped the American tobacco industry perpetuate a fraud of epic proportions on American consumers. Advertisers were in the thick of this fraud. In addition to offering up false promises about the health benefits of cigarette smoking, advertisers reinforced popular cultural understandings about "authentic Indians" existing in the past, indigenous relics frozen in time by the forces of colonial conquest. For instance, the use of tobacco-store Indians carved out of wood began a crude form of advertising that dates back to the seventeenth century. These tobacco-store Indians, also known as cigar-store Indians were ubiquitous among tobacco retailers during the nineteenth and twentieth centuries.[38]

The cigar-store Indian represented what white Americans imagined to be the "authentic Indian." Authentic Native Americans were assumed to be a dying race, so the cigar-store Indian represented a distant historical figure: the "noble savage." This creation of Western culture represented an exotic yet comfortably distant figure. Noble he may have been, but a relic of the past he was nonetheless. In this way, the cigar-store Indian reinforced the triumphalism embedded in American patriotism and popular notions of the United States as an exceptional nation.[39] Numerous cigar-store Indians across the United States were produced by different artists in different years; nevertheless, they had many common features. The wood provided the Indian figure with a bronze-colored skin. He frequently wore feather headdresses, loin clothes, moccasins, and other stereotypical types of dress. In many cases these figures seem stoic, implying the "nobility" of the noble savage, but in other cases they hold spears or other weapons, reminding patrons of the warlike savageness of Native Americans. In short, the authentic cigar-store Indian was about as inauthentic a creation as one can imagine.

The tobacco industry's commodification of Native American imagery provided a template for forgetting the long history of anti–Native American violence, forced removal, and assimilation efforts. Instead, advertisers used a contrived series of images to construct authentic Native Americans. The use of Native Americans in tobacco advertising emphasized noble, or royal, characteristics. Popular at the turn of the nineteenth and twentieth centuries were images of "Indian princesses" on tobacco trading cards and posters. As the female alternative to the male cigar-store Indian's nobility and stoic bearing, the Indian princess lived in harmony with nature. She typically had a smiling face, comely figure, and Caucasian lips that invited men into stores. The cigar-store Indian princess was an exotic "other," but she also represented wholesomeness and virginity designed to appeal to a male clientele. As one scholar observes, the Indian princess "comforts white men … promised much, [and yet] she remains aloof."[40] The imagery of the Indian princess was used to sell everything from "Indian Queen hair dye" to tobacco products during the nineteenth and twentieth centuries.[41]

The use of Native American stereotypes did not escape the attention of leading Native Americans. During the 1930s, Arthur C. Parker complained: "If the educated Indian or persons of Indian blood have no more stamina than to continue to play the carved wooden 'cigar store Indian' to sell tobacco for another man's profit—he is poorly educated indeed."[42] Such protests, however, often fell on deaf ears in white America. Like the noble savage, the Indian princess, both fantasies of Western culture, became fixtures of American popular culture by the early twentieth century. For tobacco advertisers, however, the exploitation of images of bare-breasted Native American women, surrounded by an exotic kingdom, served them well. Such imagery brought the orientalist imagery commonly associated with the Middle East and Asia home, albeit at a safe historical distance.

Also kept at a safe historical distance was the imagery of violence involving Native Americans. The historical violence perpetrated by European and European American settlers against Native Americans from the seventeenth to the twentieth century was rarely, if ever, portrayed in tobacco advertisements. Instead, "Indian warriors" featured prominently. These images drew inspiration from newspaper reports from the Plains Indian Wars and from popular entertainment, such as Buffalo Bill Cody's Wild West Show. In 1885, for example, Warpath Tobacco packaged its brand using the imagery of Native American warriors advancing on an unseen enemy. The Native American warriors appear on horseback, feathers attached to their hair, with one warrior at the center of the packaging holding a hatchet aloft.[43]

If the advertisements for Warpath Tobacco kept Native American warriors at a safe historical and geographic distance from tobacco consumers in American cities and towns, other products attempted to use humor to appeal to consumers. Personal hygiene products became particularly popular among Americans during the late nineteenth century. As was the

Images of Native Americans were frequently used to sell tobacco products. Here, Warpath Tobacco utilized the stereotypical savage Indian warrior to sell tobacco. (Library of Congress)

case with advertisements for soap, racial humor was a common feature of such advertising. Hair care products were no exception. Take, for example, "Dr. Scott's Electric Hair Brush." The prominent reference to medical bona fides offered the consumer a clue to the effectiveness of this product, which claimed to rid individuals of dandruff. With the manufacturer's medical authority established, the consumer was further convinced of the electric hairbrush's effectiveness through reference to the practice of scalping, something Europeans and European Americans associated with what they saw as the uncivilized nature of indigenous people. The caption reads, Dr. Scott's brush "will not save an Indian's scalp from his enemies but it will preserve yours from dandruff, baldness, falling hair." As a bonus, the product also promised to offer a remedy for "headache and neuralgia."

Images of Asians/Asian Americans and Mexican Americans in Advertising

During the nineteenth and twentieth centuries, trading cards emerged as one of the cheaper and more commonly used forms of mass-market advertising. Manufacturers and retailers placed trading cards on the corner of store counters. The cards were free, brightly colored, and usually targeted women and children. On one side of the card, a product was advertised; on the other, an image that appealed to the era's sensibilities for humor or leisure appeared. Significantly, a culture of card swapping developed as trading cards became increasingly widespread. As a result, the imagery on both sides of the card had the potential to reach a large audience at relatively little cost to the manufacturer on retailer.[44]

While caricatured images of African Americans and Native Americans routinely appeared on trading cards, other racial and ethnic stereotypes were exploited to advertise products. Asian American bodies, for instance, were routinely displayed on these trading cards. Advertisers often used variants on the racially derogatory term "Chinaman," rather than Chinese man, to exploit anti-Chinese sentiment among white consumers. These types of cards became particularly popular during spikes in anti-Asian and anti-immigrant hysteria during the late nineteenth and early twentieth centuries. Such cards often portrayed a demonic-looking "Chinaman" whose actions and/or words juxtaposed his working in food service or dry cleaning stores with the racial assumption that "Orientals" spread disease and dirt through the consumption of vermin, illicit narcotics, or the insinuation of sexual excess.[45]

In addition to visual stereotypes, popular racial expressions about the Oriental appeared in American advertisements. For instance, during the 1910s the Natural Food Company of New York promoted its shredded wheat using images that juxtaposed an elderly Japanese gentleman in traditional attire and a young Japanese man marching in military uniform. Borrowing from a popular saying at the time, the slogan read: "The Plucky Little Jap."[46] In the wake of Japan's defeat of Russia in the Russo-Japan war (1904–1905), this expression gained widespread use in American culture. However, it also highlighted a racial problem that eugenicists and demographers routinely emphasized: the alleged decline in the world's white races as the colored races of the world rapidly increased their numbers. Exploiting this popular racial anxiety, the Natural Food Company offered a not too subtle piece of advice to consumers: shredded wheat could contribute to the building of a "sturdy and industrious race."

Because of the long-standing presence of Asian, especially Chinese, immigrants in the American laundry industry, clothes washing took on special meaning in relations to media depictions of washermen. Chinese men were frequently the butt of jokes about laundries in the late nineteenth century. A good example comes from the 1880s' print ads for Magic Washer's liquid washing compound. In a print ad reminiscent of American propaganda broadsides, an Uncle Sam kicks a stereotypically appearing Chinese man in the backside as several other "Chinamen" flee. The caption for the ad reads, "The Chinese Must Go. We have no use for them since we got this wonderful washer [soap]." The Chinese in this ad have exaggerated features: long queues, overly slanted eyes, clawed hands, and appear almost demonic.

Along with laundries, Americans also fretted about Asians, again especially the Chinese, in the food services. In particular, while Americans came to love Chinese food, they worried about the types of meat that went into this cuisine. In about 1900, Rough on Rats pest control formula capitalized on these anxieties. The company produced a large-scale print ad to advertise its product, which "clears out rats, mice, bed bugs, flies, and roaches." That's all well and good, but it was the depiction of the Asian figure on the ad that stands out. A Chinese-looking man, wearing stereotypical Asian clothing and a conical hat, with a long queue, slanted eyes, and a bestial, almost snakelike mouth, is in the process of consuming a whole rat. He holds another rat in his free hand. The ad features the phrase, "They must go," alluding to both the rats and the Asians.

Racial stereotypes about Asian and/or Asian Americans continued to appear in American advertisements during the latter half of the twentieth century. Caricatures of the Japanese appeared with much frequency during the war years as part of the American propaganda effort. The anti-Japanese sentiment, however, continued after World War II. For instance, Revere Copper and Brass Incorporated, which had been a major manufacturer of munitions during the war, began producing items such as wheelchairs for disabled veterans. One advertisement for these products pictured a veteran sitting in a wheelchair, his right leg amputated below the knee, and the caption reading: "The Japs aren't as cross-eyed as you think."[47]

As large numbers of Americans began challenging racial discrimination and ethnic stereotypes during the 1950s and 1960s, caricatures of Asians continued to play prominent roles in marketing everything from food items to cleaning products. In the 1960s, the Rice Council of America promoted its industry with the slogan: "Did you ever see a fat Chinese?" Pillsbury promoted a range of "Funny-Face Drinks" during children's television programs in the 1960s. The beverages involved adding water to a sugar-based powder and came in a number of different flavors, such as "Injun Orange" and "Chinese Cherry."

Jell-O also attempted to appeal to children during the 1960s when it ran a television commercial using a voiceover with a stereotypical Asian accent and a cartoon depicting a "small, Chinese type baby waiting for desert" sitting in a highchair. The advertisement depicts the baby's mother "bling baby" Jell-O, a "famous Western delicacy." The "Chinese baby," however, is unable to tell which of the many flavors of Jell-O he has sitting in front of him. As the images show, and the voiceover explains, the Chinese baby is unable to taste the Jell-O because he cannot consume the product with his chopsticks. Chinese baby is saved from his plight when his mother "blings Chinese baby great Western invention, spoon. Spoon was invented for eating Jell-O." The commercial ends with the Chinese baby feeling "vely happy."

Such advertisements reduced the humanity of Asian American people to objects of ridicule.[48] But "Orientals" were not the only racialized and/ or immigrant group to be exploited by American advertisers.[49] Advertisers tended to depict Mexican-origin people and other Latinos less frequently, but ads still caricatured them.[50] As the old saying went, Mexican Americans were the "invisible minority," and that obscuration meant that they were simply ignored. When they were depicted, however, common Latino stereotypes pervaded such advertisements. These included the perception of laziness, the alleged criminality of Mexican Americans, and the exotic "hot" Latina.

One of the most glaringly obvious stereotypical portrayals of Mexican Americans came from a string of Sanka Coffee print advertisements that began to appear in newspapers and magazines in the 1940s. These ads featured a rotund, greasy-looking "Hispanic" individual who wears a large sombrero and appears quite lazy. He has come to be known as the "Juan, the Sanka Mexican." He also spoke in broken English and loved his Sanka because it was "97% caffein [sic] free," allowing him to enjoy his cup of Joe and still have a siesta. The most prolific appearance of the Sanka Mexican was a large advertisement that read much like a comic book, with different scenes designed to tell the overall story. In the first scene, Juan explains, "Everyone takes the siesta in the heat of the day, except I, poor Juan. While all are asleep, the shops are closed. Except my shop, where I sell pottery to the American tourists for ten times what it costs in America." An American woman visits his shop and asks why Juan does not take a siesta like the rest of his countrymen, many of whom are displayed in the background passed out in the streets with their sombreros pulled down over their faces. "I cannot sleep!" Juan explains, "It is the coffee!" While the tourist comments that it is good business to be open while others are napping, Juan insists, "I would give all the beezness for a good *siesta*!" She then reveals the wonders of Sanka and, "in gratitude I charge her only *five* times what the pottery is worth. Later I try Sanka Coffee. Delicious. And I *sleep* each day during the afternoon. My pottery beezness, he is ruin but *ah, amigo* … how I enjoy the *siesta*!" The ad ends with Juan slumped against his store counter, with his sombrero pulled down over his eyes, asleep.

Numerous visual and cultural stereotypes emerge from these Sanka ads. Juan's appearance is about as stereotypical as they come. He's got the sombrero, the wispy facial hair, large belly, bolo tie, and buckteeth. His central problem is that his love of caffeinated coffee interferes with his ability to be lazy and enjoy a siesta. He is also a cheat, charging exorbitant prices for his pottery, and he lowers his excessive prices slightly only for the American tourist who helps him reclaim his laziness. He speaks English poorly and calls his business "beezness." And of course, by the end of the ad he is lazily sleeping, as all Mexicans evidently are wont to do, with his sombrero pulled over his face. Mind you, Sanka also found numerous other ethnic groups to ridicule with their ads, including Russians, Jews, African Americans, and Irish people.

Racist depictions of Latinos before the 1960s are generally difficult to find. Occasionally, as with Sanka, Mexican-origin people found themselves the subjects of scorn and ridicule on a piecemeal, sporadic basis, but caricatures of this community appeared less frequently, unlike those that depicted blacks and Native Americans. This changed in the 1960s and 1970s as the Latino population, especially Mexican Americans, grew. The single best example of this type of advertising came from Frito-Lay's "Frito Bandito" ads.

The Frito Bandito was introduced in 1967. He featured a Speedy Gonzales–like appearance that included a large sombrero, wispy mustache, a white pantsuit, large buckteeth, one of which was gold, two revolvers, and two bandoliers. He speaks in broken English. He is, in short, a fairly standard depiction of a Mexican "bandit" who, in this example, seeks to do nothing more than steal Fritos corn chips. The elements of his appearance will sound familiar when the reader reaches our cartoon chapter, because the Bandito was animated by Tex Avery, one of the most prolific racist cartoon animators in American history, and was voiced by Mel Blanc.

Frito Bandito print ads often featured the character on a wanted poster. In one of these posters, the Bandito appears as if in a mug shot and the ad warns "caution: he loves crunchy Fritos corn chips so much he'll stop at nothing to get yours. What's more, he's cunning, clever—and sneaky!" The ad further warns "citizens" to protect themselves. In one poster we can see all of the common racial stereotypes about Mexican-descent people. The Bandito is, obviously, a thief, albeit a cunning, clever one. Since he prefers to steal, one can also assume he is lazy, another common stereotype about Mexican Americans. The ad also offers the line about citizens needing to protect themselves, which clearly defines the Frito Bandito as not a citizen but as an undocumented immigrant. The ad is also filled with bullet holes. The Frito Bandito appeared in other print ads in which he spoke. In one, he offers children the chance to get free coloring pencils. He entices them with the words "keeds! Free coloring pencils." The pencils are for a drawing contest; the first prize is a trip to Mexico.

The most significant Frito Bandito ads were cartoon television commercials. In one early commercial, a crudely drawn Bandito explains to the audience that the "Frito Bureau of Investigation" is after him because he is "a bad man" for stealing Frito's. He then asks the audience who has Frito's in their possession, draws his revolvers, and steals the Frito's while faux Mexican music and ricocheting bullet noises are heard. In other ads, the Bandito riffs on the popular tune "Cielito Lindo" (more commonly known as the "canta y no llores" song). In one of these commercials, he approaches the screen to ask children if they too are "Frito Banditos." If so, then they should sing along to the tune "Ay, ay, ay, ay! oh, I am dee Frito Bandito, hee

hee! I like Frito's Corn Chips. I love them, I do. I want Frito's corn chips. I'll get (or 'take' in other versions) them, from you!" In other commercials, the Frito Bandito pretends to be a parking attendant on the moon and charges astronauts Frito's for parking; in another he's a magician who turns the audience's Frito's into his Frito's. All of these ads conclude with a white actor, usually a male child or a teenage boy, enjoying some Frito's, and as he eats them, a cartoon wispy mustache is superimposed on his face.

The Frito Bandito ad campaign came to an end in the early 1970s, the result of the changing times and pressure from Mexican American advocacy groups who disliked the racist depictions inherent in these commercials. The Bandito played on common stereotypes about Mexican-descent people, especially their perceived laziness and criminality. It is interesting to note that while the Mexican-like Frito Bandito stole Frito's, many Mexican Americans consider Frito's as having been stolen from the Mexican community. The original recipe for the chips was acquired by San Antonio businessman Elmer Doolin, who purchased the recipe for the chips from Gustavo Olguin in 1932 for $100. Considering the billions of dollars Frito's has gone on to make, many Mexican Americans wonder who the Frito Bandito actually was—a cartoon caricature of Mexican-origin people, or a white man named Elmer?

Even after the failure of the Frito Bandito advertising campaign, other companies continued to utilize similar stereotypical depictions of Mexican-origin people. While tequila was not widely consumed by Americans before the late 1960s, the advocacy of the Chicano movement, which promulgated a type of cultural nationalism that popularized many Mexican foodstuffs, especially tequila, opened the floodgates for expanded tequila sales in the United States. Marketers responded with ads that, much like the Frito Bandito or the Sanka Mexican, caricatured Mexicans as bestial bandits. Take the 1975 ad campaign by Tequila Gavilan which featured a greasy Mexican-looking man with a sombrero and a bandolier of bullets across his chest. His appearance would seem to approximate a latter-day Pancho Villa, but the individual in the ad also has a stupid, drunk look to his face. He is seated while an attractive woman stands next to him. The caption for this print ad reads "Tequila Gavilan, one taste … and you're not a gringo anymore" (and if you ordered quickly you could receive a small salt shaker in the form of a. 45 caliber bullet). While it is difficult to tell, both the man and the woman appear to be non-Latinos, most likely European Americans, who have been transformed by this tequila, hence the caption. As such, we have the added element of a Latinoface depiction here. But as with other similar advertisements, all the necessary stereotypical elements appear in this advertisement. He is the timeworn bandito, a lazy, tequila drinking fool, while she is the hot, exotic Latina. Such depictions continue to afflict Latinos and Latinas today.

Conclusion

Comedian Bill Hicks once joked with his audience that anyone in advertising and marketing should "kill themselves."[51] Hicks was commenting on advertisers' greed, but he could well have been discussing their historic racism. As we have discussed, the advertising industry assists clients in marketing and selling products. But advertisers themselves also create images that consumers imbibe and ultimately believe in. They create those images, in numerous instances, out of whole cloth, but just as surely advertisers reflect broader social norms and ideas, regurgitating to the American public what they already think, know, or believe. The advertising industry's use of race and racist imagery certainly fits this pattern. Marketers' "commodity racism"[52] and the cultural process of a racist "cosmopolitan domesticity" informed the American public regarding how they should perceive people of color. Many of these racist motifs were already well established in the nineteenth century, providing advertisers ready-made tropes with which to caricature nonwhites for profit motives. The black Mammy or Sambo, the conniving untrustworthy Chinaman, the lazy Mexican, the noble savage all of these stereotypical depictions predated the rise of the advertising industry. Add to these images the "orientalism" of the era, the aforementioned Turkish curtains or "Oriental" rugs, and one can begin to appreciate the range and impact of the advertising industry's racism.[53]

The use of these stock racial depictions demonstrates one of the key ways in which racism became institutionalized in the American popular media. Advertisers communicated with numerous people, far more than book publishers—one of the other quintessential parts of a racist American media—could ever hope to reach. Because of their range, through print media of all forms, broadsides, posters, billboards, radio commercials, television advertisements, and product placement in motion pictures, advertisers communicated to mass audiences a racist vision to the American people. Their efforts were later picked up by other forms of popular media—movies and cartoons, for instance—which then rebroadcast these images in new forms and in new mediums to the U.S. population.

Chapter 3

Screening Intolerance

Few forms of popular culture shaped the historical consciousness of twentieth-century Americans as profoundly as motion pictures. Among the most enduring racial stereotypes to appear on movie screens were Hollywood's representation of conniving and diseased Asians, feckless "negroes," savage and bloodthirsty "Injuns," and the *bandido* stereotype that caricatured Latinos in film after film. These stereotypes reinforced racial assumptions about America's white supremacist history and naturalized both the institutional and popular forms of racism directed at African Americans, Asian Americans, Native Americans, and Latinos.[1] The industry's cultural impact, financial success, and celebrity of its leading performers made (and continues to make) Hollywood one of the most influential institutional forces in the United States. At the core of this influence was, as our analysis reveals, a heavy reliance on racial and racist stereotypes that both reinforced preexisting prejudices and helped to normalize cultures of white supremacy, patriarchy, and xenophobia.

In this chapter we explore media racism in the filmmaking industry. The advent of motion pictures, first in the silent film era and later in the "talkie" period, saw many of the most common and well-established racist depictions and caricatures of blacks, Native Americans, Asian Americans, and Latinos repeated on the big screen. Indeed, some of the first films produced in the United States dealt with racist themes. Like the advertising industry, films brought racism to a massive audience, communicating discriminatory themes and ideas to millions of Americans and people around the world. Like writers and advertising executives, motion picture producers, directors, and companies were products of their time, and their times (before the 1960s or 1970s, at least) were racist. That they produced negative depictions of nonwhite people is perhaps not surprising. The often vehemently negative representations of ethnic minorities, the enduring nature of these depictions, and the way they worked to educate Americans about race are, perhaps, more surprising. The screening of race further demonstrates our contention that media racism became institutionalized at a very early stage.

Blackface in American Cinema

As our analysis of advertising suggested, blackface has a long and inglorious history in American popular culture. The advent of the motion picture industry at the turn of the nineteenth and twentieth centuries extended that tradition. According to historians of American cinema, actors performed in blackface during the early twentieth century for two main reasons. First, popular racial beliefs suggested that white women needed to be protected from the insatiable sexual appetites of black men and should therefore only perform alongside white men in blackface. Second, most white Americans in Jim Crow America considered blackness to be so monstrous that the only safe and culturally palatable way to deal with it was to signify blackness with blackface actors. In other words, the leading figures in the movie industry viewed blackness as such an extreme form of racial otherness that to use African American actors to represent blackness risked turning white audiences away because the radical alterity of blackness would be lost to the human (and humane) representation of African American people.[2]

From the beginning of the motion picture industry in the United States, blackface emerged as a staple of filmmaking. In 1903, for example, a mechanic by the name of Edwin S. Porter decided to try his hand at making movies. Porter made a 12-minute movie titled *Uncle Tom's Cabin*. In Harriet Beecher Stowe's famous 1852 novel, *Uncle Tom's Cabin*, racial caricatures of mammies and "pickaninnies" punctuate the plotline. The main character, Uncle Tom, appears as a noble and long-suffering slave. Through Uncle Tom, Stowe aimed to humanize slaves and shine a light on their suffering. In contrast, Porter's Uncle Tom, played by a white actor in blackface, represents the "good Negro" of early twentieth-century cinema. Despite being enslaved, beaten, harassed, and routinely insulted, Uncle Tom remains a good and loyal slave.[3]

If blackness constituted the most radical alterity of whiteness in Jim Crow America, better that racial otherness was contained in the form of simple-minded, happy, and loyal African American characters. In this way, American cinema played an important role in reinforcing the culture of white supremacy that undergirded Jim Crow segregation. A long list of racialized (and racist) characters appeared in blackface to reinforce such common sense notions about race. From the mammy to the jezebel, watermelon-eating pickaninnies, "tragic mulattoes," loyal and obedient "Uncle Toms," and sex-crazed "bucks," all filled American movie screens during the early twentieth century. While a small and dedicated group of African American filmmakers—most notably Oscar Micheaux—made silent films that tested audience responses to topics such as racism, interracial sex, and mixed-race identity, such films were rarely seen by audiences outside of black communities in cities like New York and Chicago.[4]

Few films of the silent era captured white America's antipathy for blackness quite as spectacularly as D. W. Griffith's *Birth of a Nation* (1915). Based on Thomas Dixon Jr.'s novel *The Clansmen* (1905), *Birth of a Nation* recreated the tumult and drama of the Civil War and Reconstruction era.[5] The film centers on two families, the pro-Union (and northern) Stonemans—Austin Stoneman (Ralph Lewis), a character based on Congressman Thaddeus Stevens, his two sons, and daughter Elsie (Lillian Gish)—and the southern pro-Confederate Cameron family—which included daughters Margaret (Miriam Cooper) and Flora (Mae Marsh), and three sons, most notably Ben (Henry Walthall).

In part one of the film, the Stoneman brothers visit the Camerons on their South Carolina plantation. During this visit, Phil Stoneman (Elmer Clifton), the eldest of the two sons, falls in love with Margaret Cameron. Developing the representation of northern and southern whites falling in love across sectional and political lines, Ben Cameron becomes infatuated with Elsie Stoneman. The love match, however, is put on hold as the Civil War breaks out and the men enlist to fight for their respective sections. The following scenes are melodramatic, serving to highlight the injustice committed against the South by the Union Army and their African American allies during the war. For example, black militiamen (in blackface) under the command of a morally suspect white leader ransack the Cameron house and terrorize the Cameron women. Confederate soldiers, passing the vicinity of the Cameron plantation, save the house and women from the marauding black militia.

Such scenes presented the South, and southern men, in a noble and redemptive light. Other examples of southern male honor contextualize the first half of the film. In stark contrast to the crazed blackface militias, Ben Cameron is represented as a model of southern masculinity as he distinguishes himself at the Siege of Petersburg. Wounded in battle, Ben earns himself the nickname of "the Little Colonel" and is reunited with Elsie Stoneman, who is working as a nurse, when he is admitted to a military hospital. But the reuniting of Elsie and Ben is but a harbinger of dark days to come. The conclusion of part one and the opening scenes of part two depict President Lincoln's assassination, thus ending what Griffith perceived as the federal government's conciliatory policy toward the South and ushering in an era of "Negro rule."

Part two of *Birth of a Nation* both builds on the theme of "Negro rule" and develops a plotline in which such rule seems unnatural and dangerous to white southerners. To underscore these points, the audience's attention is drawn to Silas Lynch, a psychotic, sex-crazed, power-hungry "mulatto," who also happens to be Austin Stoneman's protégé. Stoneman (Ralph Lewis) and Lynch (played by George Siegmann in blackface) arrive in South Carolina in 1871 to observe that state's reconstruction. Amid scenes of African American voter fraud, an almost totally black state legislature containing African American representatives who are drunk, asleep at their desks, or engaged in wild scenes of squabbling, the rumblings of the white South rising again are depicted on the silver screen. The Reconstruction-era South is a world turned upside down, and Ben Cameron determines to do something about it by forming the Ku Klux Klan.

Griffith portrayed the Ku Klux Klan as the saviors of the white race and of southern civilization. This point is made in stark detail when a sex-crazed, power-hungry union captain named Gus (played by Walter Long in blackface) pursues one of Ben Cameron's sisters, Flora. Gus lusts after Flora, but Flora, a paragon of white feminine virtue, refuses his advances. In one of the more dramatic scenes of the film, Gus follows Flora as she walks to get water. Confronted by the lecherous "mulatto," Flora reiterates her refusal to submit to Gus's advances and, when pressed by Gus, dramatically throws herself off a cliff and to her death—a self-sacrificing act designed to underscore the determination of southern white women to preserve their racial purity. In response to his sister's suicide, Ben Cameron rallies the Klan. After capturing and putting Gus on trial, Gus's lifeless body is deposited on Lynch's doorstep by the Klan. It is a telling scene, one designed to highlight how the Ku Klux Klan was about to redeem the South from the corruption of "Negro rule," rid southern states of the influence of white northerners like Austin Stoneman (who flees to the North), and restore "Brotherly Love" and peace with the uniting of white northerners and southerners in marriage as in political rule.

Birth of a Nation spoke to white audiences who had become tired of the so-called Negro problem. Griffith shared these views, just as he believed the Reconstruction era had been a failed attempt at "Negro rule." But Griffith also shared with Thomas Dixon, the author of the novel on which Griffith based his film, a belief that their artistic creations were accurate historical re-creations of the Civil War and Reconstruction eras. For Griffith, transforming Dixon's novel into a motion picture was a profoundly important task. On one hand, Dixon presented audiences with a perspective on American history that was manifestly sympathetic to the South. On the other hand, he hoped to use the events of history to legitimate the nascent film industry and undermine those in American society who contended that motion pictures threatened the moral fabric of American society.[6] In Griffith's hands, cinema would become an educational tool for the masses. As Griffith declared in a 1915 interview, "The time will come when the children in the public schools will be taught practically everything by moving pictures. Certainly they will never be obliged to read history again."[7]

According to film scholar Donald Bogle, Griffith's films were not simply pro-southern in sympathies, but profoundly racist. *Birth of a Nation* was both. Griffith belonged to a long tradition of American entertainers who portrayed blackface characters in ways designed to signify the dominant white ideas about the racial inferiority of African Americans. Griffith's portrayal of black inferiority reflected the spectrum of early twentieth-century racism. In Griffith's films, blackface characters portrayed loyal and contented slaves on one end of this spectrum, and on the other, they were sex-obsessed and politically corrupt (and corruptible) "mulattoes." In between these polarities, Bogle observes that blackface characters in Griffith's films dance, sing, drink to excess, and engage in overly emotive displays of religious faith.[8]

While African American organizations such as the National Association for the Advancement of Colored People (NAACP) protested the demeaning representation of black people in *Birth of a Nation*, Griffith's film played a major role in reinforcing the idea in American popular culture that the South fought the Civil War to defend the principle of state's rights, and endured the corruption and violence of the Reconstruction era. As Hollywood transitioned from silent to talking movies, these popularly held notions about American history were further perpetuated by films that romanticized the slave South. Few films achieved this romanticization as effectively as *Gone with the Wind* (1939).

Based on Margaret Mitchell's 1936 novel of the same title, *Gone with the Wind* was the epic tale of Scarlett O'Hara (Vivien Leigh) who lives on a sprawling cotton plantation, called "Tara," in Georgia. Set against the backdrop of the Civil War, O'Hara lives a life seemingly oblivious to the sufferings of the slaves who toil on Tara—in fact, the slaves on the O'Hara plantation are portrayed as happy, content, and loyal—and the political divisions that have wrenched the nation apart seem worlds away. Scarlett O'Hara's attention is consumed by her romantic feelings for Ashley Wilkes (Leslie Howard), who, O'Hara learns, is to marry his cousin, Melanie Hamilton (Olivia de Havilland) at the nearby plantation of Twelve Oaks. It is at the reception party for Wilkes and his soon-to-be-wife that O'Hara encounters Rhett Butler (Clark Gable), a man disowned by his own family and who declares that the South has no chance if war breaks out.

Despite incurring the wrath of partygoers who insist the South can triumph in a war against the North, it is Butler's vision of the Civil War's course that turns out to be correct. Indeed, it is his chivalry that saves Scarlett O'Hara from the war's fires, as General William Tecumseh Sherman's Union Army burns Atlanta on its famous march through the South. With Butler's help, O'Hara is able to return to "Tara" and ultimately plays a pivotal role in nursing the plantation back to health despite the imposition of rising Reconstruction-era taxes, violence, and the threat of rape that follows white women as black soldiers police the South.

Gone with the Wind attracted intense criticism from African American organizations and scholars. The dramatist Carlton Moss famously quipped that if *Birth of a Nation* constituted a "frontal attack on American history and the Negro people," *Gone with the Wind* was a "rear attack on the same."[9] Like many other African American scholars and political leaders, Moss viewed *Gone with the Wind* as a piece of cinematic nostalgia, designed to feed the mythology of the Lost Cause that now dominated popular perceptions of the Civil War and Reconstruction eras and that sympathized with slavery by presenting the North as overly aggressive and slaves as loyal and contented. The film's leading African American star, Hattie McDaniel, played the O'Hara's loyal "Mammy." Her portrayal earned her the ire of the NAACP's Walter White, but it also won her rave reviews from the *New York Times* and ultimately an academy award for her portrayal of the loyal, if opinionated, Mammy.[10] Indeed, McDaniel's performance in *Gone with the Wind* would no doubt have been instantly recognizable to audiences familiar with advertisements for Aunt Jemima's pancakes. Like Aunt Jemima, McDaniel's Mammy in *Gone with the Wind* was, to borrow from one scholar, an "omnipresent, cow-like, asexual, obese provider—eternally associated with biscuit dough."[11]

If McDaniel's portrayal of "Mammy" in *Gone with the Wind* placed the image of the loyal black slave in front of twentieth-century movie audiences, McDaniel's subsequent roles presented in caricature form of other aspects of the "Mammy" motif. For example, in *Maryland* (1940), McDaniel's character was jolly; in films like *Margie* (1946), McDaniel's Mammy character was unflinchingly loyal; and in *Song of the South* (1946), McDaniel's character is cheerful.[12]

Birth of a Nation and *Gone with the Wind* are two of the most popular films that used stock racial motifs and racist themes. Of course, hundreds of other films dealt with similar racist concepts. These included the black-blackface portrayals of lazy, indolent blacks by actors such as Lincoln Theodore Monroe Andrew Perry and William Best, both better known by their stage names "Stepin Fetchit" and "Eat and Sleep," respectively. The two characters greatly mirrored one another, with both Perry and Best caricaturing African Americans by acting in a dimwitted, lazy fashion. The two were often barely able to rouse themselves from bed, they both spoke in a slow drawl that further demarcated their lack of intelligence, and they seemed to live in dire, poverty-stricken circumstances, although neither seemed bothered by this in their films. Interestingly, offscreen Perry was the mirror opposite of his Stepin Fetchit alter ego. He was well educated, wrote for newspapers such as the *Chicago Defender*, and was not poor nor lazy. The Stepin Fetchit–type character continued to find expression in Hollywood, from cartoon depictions such as "Tex's Coon" in the famous banned short "All This and Rabbit Stew" to "Buckwheat" in *The Little Rascals*.

By the Cold War decades of the late 1940s and 1950s, Hollywood continued to make films that portrayed African Americans in stereotypical ways. However, a number of these films evinced a concern for changing social attitudes about race in the United States. Blackface characters had fallen out of favor in Hollywood films, but loyal Mammies and Uncle Toms remained. But such characters were also becoming less common by the late 1940s. In their place, Hollywood filmmakers produced "problem films," movies that attempted to delve into the complexities of racial mixing and mixed-race identities.

In the context of Hollywood producing such racist films as *Birth of a Nation* and *Gone with the Wind*, problem films were a significant advance in the way Hollywood presented race and racism. Films such as *Lost Boundaries* (1949) confronted the sociological significance of "passing" and mixed-race identity. Trapped between the white and black worlds, mixed-race families—or "tragic mulattoes"—faced what filmmakers perceived as a moral choice about whether they should pass as white (if their skin color allowed such a decision) or embrace their racial mixture. Such films strove to engender understanding—to "connect" with the "other," as one scholar puts it—for the emotional struggles (the madness, despair, and depression) that Hollywood filmmakers imagined mixed-race families went through.[13]

Critical to Cold War–era problem films was finding a solution to the issues posed by a movie's plot.[14] The makers of problem films recognized that racial prejudices caused mixed-race couples, people, and families emotional and social hardships. Overcoming such hardships required a type of humanist leap of faith, a recognition that all human beings constitute a single human species. Few films attempted to preach such racial understanding to audiences quite as explicitly as *Guess Who's Coming to Dinner*. Set against the backdrop of the desegregation of public schools, the civil rights movement, and the rise of Black Power in the late 1960s, *Guess Who's Coming to Dinner* was a film that did not foretell social chaos, as racial alarmists in the South warned, but challenged audiences to confront the racially mixed nature of the American population.[15] True to Hollywood form, the film broached a far-reaching social issue by framing it in personalized terms, specifically through the cinematic device of an interracial love story. While the film does not shy away from issues of bigotry, racism, sexism, and jealousy, the romantic tone of the film suggests inevitable historical progress will be made on this and related issues in the not-to-distant future.[16] In this way, *Guess Who's Coming to Dinner* captured the optimistic ethos of the era.

Yellowface in American Cinema

Like blackface portrayals, yellowface depictions go back to the very earliest motion pictures. Stereotypical depictions of Asians usually broke down into two main categories: for men, the evil, wily "Oriental" or the kind, wise mystic; for women, the evil, highly sexual dragon lady (the female equivalent of the evil, wily male) or the demure and delicate china doll. For the Asian male archetype, no other character better illustrates the scope and longevity of racist representations of Asian peoples than Dr. Fu Manchu. As noted in Chapter 1, English novelist Sax Rohmer originally created Fu Manchu in 1912 with the serialized publication of *The Mystery of Dr. Fu Manchu*, which came to U.S. audiences in 1913 as *The Insidious Dr. Fu-Manchu*. That story revolved around the character binary shared by Fu Manchu and the former Scotland Yard detective Denis Nayland Smith. In Rohmer's telling, Fu Manchu represented the "yellow peril" incarnate, a sinister villain with a knack for killing his opponents with rare and evil skills, especially poisoning. He is also able to harness the powers of poisonous creatures such as snakes or spiders.

Dr. Fu Manchu's first film appearance was in the British silent movie *The Mystery of Dr. Fu Manchu* (1923). The copies of this film are at this time locked in the vaults of British Film Institute (BFI). As film scholar John Soister observes, movies like *The Mystery of Dr. Fu Manchu* "haven't seen the light of the carbon arc in years." Soister attributes this to the film's lack of importance to overall cinematic history, and he could be right.[17] Just as surely, though, the BFI may well be worried about his film's racist content and has chosen not to release an offensive film. Whatever its motivation, the broad outlines of the film mirror the plot of the book. A mysterious villain, Fu Manchu, portrayed by English actor Harry Agar Lyons, in a classic yellowface depiction (despite the fact that he does not look Asian), attempts to murder his opponents in a variety of fascinating ways, from a cat with poison-tipped claws to poisoned flowers.

The bad doctor made his first appearance on American screens in *The Mysterious Dr. Fu Manchu* (1929). That film starred Warner Oland, an actor who went on to portray other yellowface characters, most notably Charlie Chan. The film opens with stereotypical sounding "Chinese" music and what appears to be a statue of a fire-breathing dragon. This scene foretells how the forces of the "white defenses of Peking," save for the British, fall to the "Oriental horde" during the Boxer Uprising of 1900. A father sends his daughter to live with his "friend" Dr. Fu, who in the early stage of this film appears to be a good guy. He also seems to have mystical powers, able to cast a hypnotic spell on the young girl, but then awakens her because "if anything should happen to me no one could waken her." Fu Manchu arouses the girl from her sleep with a magical touch and the command of "waken, Little Blossom, waken."

This scene, as with others throughout the film, portrays Chinese characters who speak in a broken, stereotypical fashion. For example, one of these stereotypical characters explains to Fu Manchu that white soldiers are nearing, "their great fire sticks belch forth death." Fu Manchu promises the young girl and another yellowface woman—who appears to be his wife—that they have nothing to fear. However, when some of the Boxers use his compound to make a last stand, the British attack, killing his wife and child. Only Dr. Fu and the young girl, "Little Blossom," survive. He vows to avenge his family and will ultimately use the young girl, later known as Lia Eltham, as his instrument for enacting revenge.

Some years later, audiences learn that Fu Manchu murdered all of the descendants of those who killed his family except for one soldier and his son. That soldier is General John Petrie and his son, Dr. James Petrie.

Unaware of her role in Fu's plot, Dr. Petrie has a chance encounter with Lia Eltham on the streets of London. Father and son Petrie shortly after this chance meeting receive a visit from detective Nayland Smith, who explains that they've become the target of a sinister "fiend" who has been "systematically poisoning the officers of the Boxer Rebellion." The general sneers at these warnings, only to be quickly overcome by a cloud of poisonous gas as he prepares his pipe. A detective spots a shadowy figure fleeing the Petrie house, follows him to Chinatown, only to be shot by a poison dart fired from a blowgun operated by Fu Manchu's trusted servant Li Po, played by African American actor Noble Johnson. The unfortunate detective is barely able to report his location—Singapore Charlie's Bar—before dying from the poison dart. The doctor and Smith stake out the bar, and Petrie again encounters Lia Eltham. He asks for her help, and she explains that her benefactor, the great Dr. Fu Manchu, may be able to help. Thus, Petrie and Smith begin receiving aid from their nemesis. Later, when the two realize their mistake, they confront Fu Manchu, who drinks a poisoned tea intended for Petrie and dies.

As one of Hollywood's first talkies, *The Mysterious Dr. Fu Manchu* lacked the depth and flow of subsequent films. The film's narrative is plodding, and the actors, almost all veterans of the silent era, give overly contrived performances. Despite these flaws, the movie's story line is compelling and the arc of the film, especially as Smith and Petrie begin to receive aid from their enemy, is riveting. Moreover, the stereotypical depictions of yellowface characters highlight the racism embedded in the motion picture industry during its formative decades. In a film about a Chinese character that opens in China, no Chinese actors appear in the movie. Instead, every actor is in yellowface, even the one black actor, Noble Johnson, who made a career portraying whiteface and yellowface characters.[18]

Warner Oland's depiction of Fu Manchu fits in with many of the early twentieth-century stereotypes about the evil, wily Asian. The Swedish-born Oland is perhaps most convincing in his role Dr. Fu, the secretive "Oriental" with mystical powers, characteristics that his skill as a hypnotist and proficient use of poisons is meant to highlight. In fact, Eltham appears in a daze throughout most of the film because of Dr. Fu's hypnotic skills. Fu Manchu and Li Po's manipulation of poison, use of the dart gun, and control of a white woman all represent not only classic depictions within yellowface but also a classic portrayal of the yellow peril, or white America's fear about the duplicitous nature and amoral behavior of Asian people. Only the death of the protagonist, by his own hand, can right such wrongs. Of course, one of the things established by the film is that Dr. Fu Manchu is so adept at making poisonous concoctions that he can tailor them to a particular victim. As such, the film prompts audiences to puzzle over how Fu Manchu could possibly die by ingesting a poisoned tea meant for Dr. Petrie.

The critical final scene, which uses stereotypical Chinese-sounding music, presages future developments for Dr. Fu Manchu. These developments begin to be revealed to audiences in the 1930 film *The Return of Dr. Fu Manchu*. This film establishes that the poisoned tea merely put Dr. Fu into a comma-like state and he is quickly restored to his full sinister self. *The Return of Dr. Fu Manchu* opens at the bad doctor's funeral where a group of Chinese "priests," who chant in a Hare Krishna–like fashion, seal Fu Manchu in his coffin. For reasons that remain unexplained, detective Smith attends Fu Manchu's funeral. And Lia Eltham appears so distraught that Dr. Petrie escorts her away from the proceedings. The melodrama and mystery of Fu Manchu's funeral is overlaid with a reiteration of the previous movie, done through Nayland Smith giving a newspaper reporter a longwinded narration of the story of Dr. Fu Manchu. When the inspector explains how Dr. Fu died, the reporter responds by saying "ha, delightful, chap!" As Smith gives this account, a secret door in the coffin opens, and Dr. Fu escapes.

From this point forward *The Return of Dr. Fu Manchu* extends the basic plotline of *The Mysterious Dr. Fu Manchu*. Dr. Fu vows revenge for the fate that befell him and targets Dr. Petrie. We learn that Petrie and Eltham are engaged, and so there is a clumsy attempt to add an element of romance to the film. This relationship compounds the ways in which Dr. Fu provokes great fear, especially among the women of Dr. Petrie's household. The doctor is so wily that he is able to spy on the couple from a biplane and exert a measure of his hypnotic mind control over Lia from the air. Despite Fu Manchu's deception and attempts to sabotage the relationship, the wedding proceeds. It is this wedding scene that provides the dramatic stage for one of the bride's attendants to burst into the chapel to tell the audience that Fu Manchu lives. Those attending the wedding are stunned and puzzled over how Fu Manchu could be alive. Smith provides an explanation, declaring, "The poison he took was obviously … not poison." Smith adds that Fu Manchu's funeral, "conducted entirely by Orientals," was clearly a fake. Unbeknownst to the wedding guests, the Petrie home is already surrounded by Dr. Fu's forces, and Eltham is quickly kidnapped.

The Return of Dr. Fu Manchu reiterates popular racial assumptions about cunning, conniving, and secretive "Orientals." This racialized framework guides the film as it lurches toward its climactic final moments when Dr. Fu once again confronts Dr. Petrie and gives him a terrible choice. Dr. Fu proposes to either set off a grenade that will kill everyone, or have Dr. Petrie take a potion and sacrifice himself for the good of Lia Altham and Nayland Smith. Unwilling to abide by Fu Manchu's ultimatum, Dr. Petrie musters all of his strength and pushes Dr. Fu out a window and into a river. As Dr. Fu's body makes contact with the water the grenade explodes, and Fu Manchu is, presumably, dead (again).

The Return of Dr. Fu Manchu, the second in a trilogy, is clumsy and hackneyed in both its dialog and action scenes. What keeps the film, and the trilogy, together, is the racist stereotyping of Chinese people. In this sense, the use of yellowface underscores the foreignness of Asian people, an effect enhanced by Oland's yellowface performance of Dr. Fu and the utterly unrealistic Hare Krishna singing by the priests at Fu Manchu's funeral, as well as the notion that "Orientals" were so untrustworthy that of course they conspired in the faking of his death. The Hare Krishna–style singing is absurd, as there exists no basis in Chinese culture for such chanting and instead serves the film's narrative purpose of mocking Chinese culture and religion. Nonetheless, the funeral scene serves an important dramatic purpose, helping to establish that all Asians are wily and untrustworthy. Moreover, Chinese people are portrayed as savage and merciless, a stereotype conveyed by Fu and his vow to torture Lia.

The theme of savage, merciless, and hateful Asian people shades the portrayals of other yellowface characters. For example, Oland's "Chinese-like" character inverts white racial animus toward Asian people when he exclaims that white people are "white devils." Dr. Fu's servant, Cheng, is equally a Chinese stereotype. Unlike the previous film, though, Cheng is not represented in yellowface but is played by a person of Asian heritage, Japanese American character actor Tetsu Komai. Therefore, *The Return of Dr. Fu Manchu* not only reinforces a racist yellowface motif in early twentieth-century movie making but constitutes an equally racist presentation of yellow-yellowface, a form of cinematic representation that involved actors of Asian or Asian American backgrounds playing stereotypical yellowface characters.[19]

The final installment in the original Fu Manchu American trilogy is *Daughter of the Dragon* (1931). Oland's Dr. Fu, the only cast member from the previous two films, receives minimal screen time in the third film. Dr. Fu's surprisingly limited screen time aside, the film retains its racially clichéd, convoluted plotlines. What merits mention is that Chinese American actress Anna May Wong plays the titular Daughter of the Dragon (i.e., Fu Manchu). Wong, an important film star of the silent and talkie eras, frequently portrayed yellow-yellowface characters, and *Daughter of the Dragon* was one of her first major starring roles. We will return to Wong later in this chapter.

Conscious that most American audiences subscribed to the "yellow peril" fear about "hordes" of "Oriental" migrants arriving in the United States, the American filmmaking industry recognized how it could capitalize on popular prejudices by making the Fu Manchu trilogy. Indeed, once the original trilogy concluded, further Fu Manchu films were made. For example, Dr. Fu returns in probably his most famous incarnation, *The Mask of Fu Manchu* (1932). This was one of the few films produced by William Randolph Hearst's Cosmopolitan Productions and starred the legendary Boris Karloff as Fu Manchu. The film opens with Nayland Smith (played by Lewis Stone) being drawn back into his country's service after secret

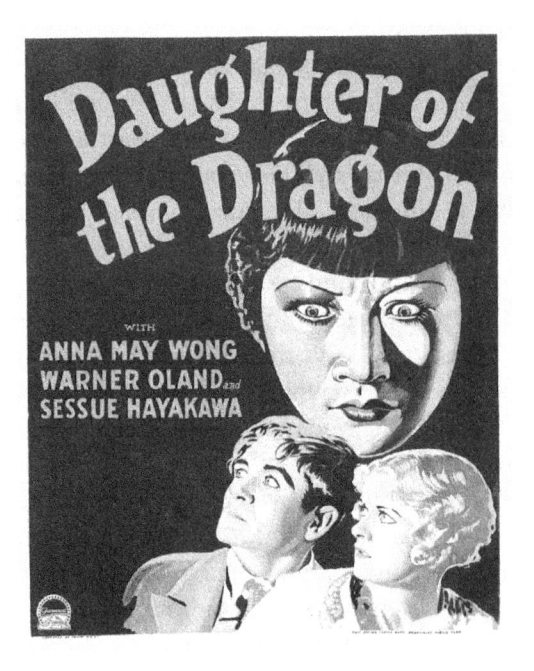

Asian Americans, if they were cast in motion pictures at all, almost always portrayed negative stereotypical versions of Asian people. In *Daughter of the Dragon*, a sinister-looking Anna May Wong stars as Fu Manchu's daughter Ling Moy in a classic yellow-yellowface performance.

agents learn that Fu Manchu aspires to locate the grave of Genghis Khan. The film's plot revolves around Fu Manchu coveting the sword and mask of Khan so that he can unite all Asian peoples against the Western world, and then, as he explains later in the film to a group of Chinese men, "conquer and breed! Kill the white man and take his women!" This transparently racist plotline follows the cultural contours of eugenic discourse in early twentieth-century politics and culture. Eugenics revolved around the idea that genetic improvements in humankind were possible when "the more suitable races or strains of blood" (i.e., white) intermingle.[20] For the popularizers of eugenics in the United States, improving the genetic qualities of humankind was routinely overshadowed by the specter of subaltern peoples—particularly "Mongolian Asiatics" and Africans—reproducing their populations at a much faster rate than Caucasians. The American eugenicist Lothrop Stoddard referred to this as the "rising tide of color," a development that promised to have not a eugenic impact on global populations, but a "dysgenic" effect.[21]

The widespread cultural appeal of such views meant that *The Mask of Fu Manchu* resonated with American audiences. The film therefore has Smith and Egyptologist Sir Lionel Barton (Lawrence Grant) joining forces to beat Fu Manchu to Genghis Khan's grave. However, Sir Lionel is kidnapped and brought to Fu Manchu, who tries to bribe Barton by offering him his daughter Fah Lo See (Myrna Loy). Fu Manchu's effort to bribe Barton fails, leading to one of the film's several torture scenes as Sir Lionel is whipped mercilessly by Fah Lo See (who is secretly attracted to Granville, giving this scene an element of sadistic bondage).

Sheila Barton (Karen Morley), Sir Lionel's daughter, takes her father's place on the expedition and with the help of her fiancé Terrence "Terry" Granville (Charles Starrett), Von Berg (Jean Hersholt), and McLeod (David Torrence) find the tomb. Their quest does not go well, with Granville being injected with a secret potion that renders him obedient to Dr. Fu. Granville then tricks the others into turning over Genghis Khan's sword and mask to Fu Manchu. Eventually Granville, Smith, and Sheila Barton, the love interest of the film, are all captured. They are all to be executed. They all escape, however, and Smith (who was placed in a room filled with alligators) ultimately uses the sword of Genghis Khan to "kill" Dr. Fu Manchu.

The Mask of Fu Manchu is characterized by its overt racism and sexualized imagery. Since the film was released before the advent of Hollywood's Motion Picture Production Code, the industry's first attempt at a type of rating system (and hence films like *The Mask of Fu Manchu* are known as Pre-Code films), the highly sexualized, violent, and racist plot elements went unremarked on by censors. Compounding the film's racism, no Asian or Asian American actors are cast in meaningful roles in this movie. Karloff does a classic yellowface depiction of Dr. Fu. Karloff's performance is rich with visual appeal, from makeup that makes his eyes appear more narrow and "slantier" than they really are to his Chinese-looking mustache and long fingernails. In addition, his mystical powers over poison, animals, and electricity (featured prominently in the film) give him supernatural abilities that Smith and the others must somehow contend with. He is meant to represent the stereotypical "hideous" "Oriental," or as Sheila calls him to his face "you hideous yellow monster!" The only "ethnic" actors in the film are Fu's henchmen, all black (or African) men wearing loincloths, who speak in grunts and who are sacrificed by the bad doctor. In one scene, for example, while Dr. Fu prepares the concoction that will give him control over Granville, he extracts venom from a snake (interestingly from a boa constrictor, which is nonvenomous) by allowing the snake to bite one of these henchmen, who is held in place by other black henchmen. The henchmen watch the doctor as he prepares the potion while the man they are holding slowly dies. As such, two ethnic groups are maligned in the film: the yellowface Chinese are evil and despotic, intent on world domination, while the blacks are mindless lackeys, easily controlled and sacrificed by their Asian captor and overlord.

The Fu Machu films served an important ideological function in early twentieth-century culture. American Studies professor Ruth Mayer explains this ideological functioning in the following way:

> The semantic and visual repertory of racism and supremacism is firmly in place in both the [Fu Manchu] novels and the films. But at the same time, the world and the people on display in these narratives are crude caricatures, fantastic concoctions, evidently made up…. These days, Fu Manchu films' exaggerated, "camp" aesthetics is often taken as an indication of their ideological harmlessness; they seem to be too far out in their exaggerated representations of the yellow-peril theme to work. I do think, however, that originally these narratives *did* work at the ideological level, and that they worked *because* of the intensity of their ascriptions and fetishistic condensations rather than in spite of it.[22]

Our analysis concurs with Mayer's conclusions. The Fu Manchu films resonated with American audiences because they touched on a key facet of the racial anxieties harbored by white Americans and perpetuated by

Hollywood. As film critic Elizabeth Kingsley sarcastically observes, "*The Mask Of Fu Manchu* Award For Jaw-Dropping Racism finally goes to neither its Asians nor its Caucasians, but to Hollywood itself."[23] The racism endemic in the original Fu Manchu films recur in the 1940 classic *Drums of Fu Manchu*, and again in the 1960s remakes of Dr. Fu Manchu. Anti-Asian racism had become so embedded in the American film industry that Fu Manchu remained a stereotypically evil, wily "Oriental." Giving white audiences a continued sense of connection with the Fu Manchu films are characters like Sheila who routinely give voice to a vicious form of racism in which the phrase "you hideous yellow monster!" reduces Asian people to the level of beasts.

The Fu Manchu films did not exercise a monopoly over Asian stereotypes in Hollywood films. Take, for example, the seemingly benign Charlie Chan. The Chan character is a classic depiction of the wise Asian who uses his much-touted mystical powers of deduction for good. Charlie Chan is, in many ways, a Chinese version of Sherlock Holmes, albeit with secretive, supernatural powers of deduction. There have been far more Charlie Chan films than Fu Manchu movies, perhaps indicating not only the draw of the character but the power of the racial archetype visible in Chan. While the evil Asian archetype has appeared in a number of late twentieth-century films, such as Dr. Yen Lo in *The Manchurian Candidate* or Ming the Merciless in the *Flash Gordon* film, we would suggest that the "good" wily Asian—ranging from the *Green Hornet*'s Kato to *The Karate Kid*'s Mr. Miyagi—became far more prolific in Hollywood films. Cinematic depictions of the "good Oriental," who was sometimes wily and always wise, began with Charlie Chan.

As we noted in Chapter 1, Charlie Chan was the creation of Earl Derr Biggers, an American author who became enamored with the work of Honolulu detective Chang Apana. Chan, who lacked the evil and conniving characteristics of Fu Manchu, made his first appearance in Biggers's 1925 novel *House without a Key*. Chan appeared briefly in that novel but returns in other Biggers's novels where he had more substantial roles. Biggers described Chan in a number of pejorative ways in his novels. These included descriptions of Chan as fat, feminine, aping of white people, assimilationist, and a yellow Uncle Tom.

These characteristics became part of Charlie Chan's film personae, made famous by the yellowface performances of Swiss actor Warner Oland.[24] Oland's rendering of the Chan character came after initial performances by Japanese actors such as George Kuwa in the 1925 silent film *House without a Key* and Sōjin Kamiyama's 1927 performance in the silent film *The Chinese Parrot*. With the advent of sound, however, almost all actors who played Charlie Chan were white, beginning with Chan's most prolific yellowface portrayer, Oland.[25]

Warner Oland's first Charlie Chan film was *Charlie Chan Carries On* (1931), produced in the same year Oland starred in his final Fu Manchu film. *Charlie Chan Carries On* is a lost film, and no copy of it is currently available for viewing. The first film of Oland playing Chan that is available is *The Black Camel* (1931). The film revolves around an actress, Shelah Fayne (played by Dorothy Revier), who is filming a motion picture in Honolulu. She's fallen for Allen Jaynes (William Post Jr.), but before she marries him she calls in an advisor, Tarneverro (Bela Lugosi), to seek his approval. But before Fayne can get that approval she winds up dead, bringing Chan into the film to investigate the homicide.[26]

Oland portrays Charlie Chan as an oafish, "rotund," but nonetheless skilled, detective. That he can pull off such a performance is testimony to Oland's acting skills, and to a long career as a yellowface performer prior to landing the Charlie Chan role.[27] In *The Black Camel*, Oland speaks in a "sing-song Chinese" voice, a voice that also entered American households in radio serials.[28] His first spoken words, to his subordinate Kashimo (Otto Yamaoka), are, "I'm pretending to be Chinese merchant, do not mention police, go way … go far away, investigate there long time." He soon meets the mysterious Tarneverro and speaks to him in an equally stereotypical way. "Have I pleasure of meeting Tarneverro the great, lifter of veils, peeker into mystery of foocher [future]?" Tarneverro responds in the affirmative, prompting Chan to exclaim, "Like shadow follows man, so fame has followed you from Hollywood."

In these scenes Chan is posing as "humble Chinese merchant," but he's so bad at it that Tarneverro quickly sees through his deception. In fact, these scenes capture how Oland's Chan is so compulsively polite that he frequently seems confused and befuddled. Chan is also, however, a smart and capable detective, albeit in an effete manner that hints at his racial and sexual "otherness." With these qualities to draw on, Chan is able to solve the film's homicide. Interestingly, Kashimo, Chan's subordinate, serves as comic relief, the foil to Chan's intellect and crime-solving nous. Kashimo is frequently so befuddled that he does not catch on to insults directed at him by Chan. Kashimo also runs about in an oddly goofy way—his arms don't move and he routinely rears back—adding to his overall slapstick appeal.

The Charlie Chan films featuring Oland (and subsequently Sydney Toler) in the lead role all elaborated on the themes established in the features like *The Black Camel*. Chan remains effete and occasionally appears effeminate, compliant, and even subservient to white people. In addition, Chan is poetic, who speaks broken English and spouts risible Confucian-like statements. Above all, Chan is portrayed as a good and capable detective, possessing a keen intellect and even secret intuitive powers of deduction. Therein lies the stereotype. As historian Ken Hanke observes, Chan was not portrayed as a racial threat in the manner Fu Manchu was represented, but "Charlie's greatest sin is perhaps not in himself, but in the fact that he was virtually the only positive depiction of an Oriental in film at the time."[29]

The Asian archetypes we have discussed thus far represented masculine interpretations of yellowface in early twentieth-century American cinema. Stereotypical depictions of Asian women were in many cases even more racist and sexist than yellowface representations of men. The most common racist archetypes for Asian women were the "dragon lady," and the "Madame Butterfly" or "china doll" caricatures. These representations were all racially offensive. The dragon lady stereotype focused on Asian female sexuality and deceitfulness. This archetype constitutes something of a female version of Fu Manchu. The dragon lady was mischievous, cunning, domineering, and exotic. She was often hypersexual, using her exoticness to deceive and mislead white men. The china doll archetype is the dragon lady's polar opposite. She is demure, modest, and subservient, perhaps geisha-like in a Pan-Asian way. She is also dependent, usually on a white male, and, while certainly intelligent and graceful, can be subjugated and cast aside at will. Whereas white men usually performed yellowface depictions of stereotypical Asian males, in numerous cases Asian/Asian American women portrayed the china doll and dragon lady archetypes.

One of the most prolific actresses to portray both versions of the dragon lady and the china doll was Anna May Wong.[30] She had an extensive career in the United States and was frequently perceived by American audiences as a Chinese national. In actuality, Wong was born in Los Angeles. However, Wong did leave the United States in the late 1920s because, as she put it, "I was so tired of the parts I had to play."[31] She spent many years in Germany, where German audiences also viewed her as Chinese. Wong's first major acting role in American film was in the silent-era drama *Toll of the Sea* (1922). She played "Lotus Flower," a young Chinese girl who rescues an unconscious man from the sea. He turns out to be an American named Allen Carver, and the two soon fall madly in love. The relationship has its ups and downs, and after a period of separation, Lotus Flower reveals she has a small child, Carver's son, and after some convincing Lotus Flower agrees to turn the child over to Carver and his American wife. As they depart, Lotus Flower wades into the sea and drowns.

Toll of the Sea quite clearly borrows heavily from *Madame Butterfly*. As a silent film, it relies on visual cues from the actors to convey meaning and emotion. We do not know, for example, if Lotus Flower's speaking pattern suggests softness, demurity, and/or chastity. We do know what she says, though, based on the dialog that is subtitled throughout this silent film, and that dialog is the type of racist broken English, Chinese-speak we've seen in other films. For example, after Carver plans to leave China, Lotus Flower exclaims, "Oh my husband, I love you so! If you no come to me, you make my heart go dead." Other important aspects of the china doll archetype are also present. For example, Lotus Flower is a character easy to cast off, a submissive woman who appears to willingly surrender her child so that he can be raised in the United States. Such submissiveness makes Lotus Flower a tragic figure, a characteristic conveyed to audiences when she commits suicide. Thus, Wong's Lotus Flower represents a very early portray of a female yellow-yellowface, a caricature of a Chinese character portrayed by an actress of Chinese heritage.

Wong had several other supporting screen appearances, all racist yellow-yellowface depictions of stereotypical Asians characters. In the 1923 silent film *Drifting*, for example, a story about the opium trade and the untrustworthy, inherently deceitful nature of Asian people, Wong briefly portrays a concubine. Chinese American stars like Wong often portrayed prostitutes, a role that conformed to American stereotypes about Asian women being willing to submit to the carnal desires of male suitors. In the 1924 silent film *The Thief of Bagdad*, Wong plays "the Mongol Slave." That is not a description but the actual name of her character in the film. She appears scantily clad and is the pawn of the film's star, the thief "Ahmed" (Douglas Fairbanks). His depiction is, of course, an unflinchingly racist representation of Middle Eastern people. Wong continued to portray china dolls and dragon ladies in other films and grew increasingly frustrated with these roles. She hoped to distance herself from these stereotypical characters, and thus Wong moved to Europe in 1928. As one historian observes of Wong's career, "Hollywood had typecast her as an Orientalist performer and burdened her ambitions with the prejudices of the era."[32]

Anna May Wong found success and critical acclaim in Germany. She starred in a number of films produced by German powerhouse director

Richard Eichberg, most notably *Song* (1928, titled *Schmutziges Geld* in German) and *City Butterfly* (1929, or *Großstadtschmetterling*). While Wong hoped to escape being typecast as a china doll or dragon lady, she instead portrayed German versions of the same stereotypical roles. In *Song*, for example, Wong plays the titular character, a poor Asian girl in an unnamed city who is befriended by a white benefactor named John. He is a performer who incorporates Song into his act as an exotic dancer. While she falls in love with John, his interests lie elsewhere. Only late in the film does John come to appreciate Song, to love her, and he dashes to the theater as Song is performing an especially dangerous dagger routine. Startled by John, she falls on the dagger and dies. As in her other films of this era, Wong portrays Song as a scantily clad, sexually exotic, and tragic character. She is helpless and subservient, a pawn used by John until he realizes her value, only to cause her demise in that realization. *City Butterfly* reiterates many of the same themes, with Wong's character, again an exotic dancer, befriended by a white benefactor.[33]

Anna May Wong was one of the first female Chinese American stars to learn one of Hollywood's most important lessons: most roles portraying ethnic "others" went to white actors. Hollywood, as well as the foreign film industry, preferred white stars who could approximate nonwhite characters. This dynamic served to reinforce the racial alterity of "Orientals" and to underline their danger to the (white) American republic. As such, someone like Warner Oland or Boris Karloff could best portray Asian characters in yellowface to make this point. In fact, it was yellowface that Hollywood preferred, so when an authentically Asian star like Wong came along, even she had to assume a yellowface personae, or what Yiman Wang has accurately called "yellow-yellowface." All of this meant that in Hollywood an Asian actor could, at best, hope to mimic a white example of what an "authentic" Asian character was supposed to be.[34]

Hollywood's racist representation of Asian and Asian American characters spanned the silent and talkie eras, and reinforced popular prejudices against Asian countries. From the Russo-Japan War (1904–1905) to the Japanese bombing of Pearl Harbor in Honolulu, Hawaii, on December 7, 1941, racist stereotypes of Asians remained a staple of Hollywood filmmaking. In the wake of Pearl Harbor, Hollywood filmmakers wasted little time in portraying the Japanese as fanatical, sneaky, dirty, savage, sadistic, excessively libidinous, and repulsive. In films such as *Wake Island* (1942), *Purple Heart* (1944), and *Dragon Seed* (1944), the "Japs" were portrayed in reference to these racial stereotypes. Indeed, cinematic representations of this nature continued into the late 1940s and during the Korean War in the early 1950s, with films such as *The Sands of Iwo Jima* (1949) and *Halls of Montezuma* (1951) representing the "yellow peril" of Japan and China as a "Communistic grab" for world domination.[35]

Few films captured the essence of these Cold War–era anxieties as effectively as *The Manchurian Candidate* (1962). Based on the 1959 novel of the same name by Richard Condon, *The Manchurian Candidate* is the story of a Communist scheme to brainwash and program assassins who will gun down an American politician. The film capitalized on CIA allegations that American POWs from the Korean War reported "a blank period" while held in camps across the Manchurian border and were allegedly trained to be "sleepers" (or dormant agents) when they returned to the United States.[36] Thus, the CIA appeared to have revealed a real-life Fu Manchu–like scenario in which conniving "Orientals" used hypnosis to manipulate the minds of Americans to act in ways detrimental to the American republic.

The Manchurian Candidate centers on the Soviet capture of U.S. troops during the Korean War. The soldiers are taken to Manchuria, located in Communist China, where they are hypnotized and brainwashed by the evil Dr. Yen Lo (Khigh Dhiegh). Several days after the capture and brainwashing of the American troops, they return to U.S. lines, with only two of their original number missing. Staff Sergeant Raymond Shaw (played by Laurence Harvey) is credited with saving U.S. soldiers. His platoon captain, Bennett Marco (Frank Sinatra), recommends Raymond for the Medal of Honor, claiming: "Raymond Shaw is the kindest, bravest, warmest, most wonderful human being I've ever known in my life."

In truth, Raymond Shaw is a loner and an utterly unsympathetic character. The Communist brainwashing of the American troops artificially altered this perception. However, Captain Marco experiences a recurring dream in which Shaw murders the two missing U.S. soldiers in front of military leaders from the world's Communist nations. However, Marco is only able to convince army intelligence officials to investigate allegations of Communist brainwashing after Allen Melvin (James Edwards), a fellow platoon member, has the same dream and can identify leading Communist figures.

The plotline of *The Manchurian Candidate* takes a twist when audiences learn that Shaw's mother, Eleanor Iselin (Angela Lansbury), is the American "operator" who controls Raymond. Iselin also controls the political career of her husband, Senator John Yerkes Iselin (James Gregory), a character modeled after Joseph McCarthy. Eleanor Iselin's objective is to secure the presidency and install Communist rule over the United States. With the plot put into action, it is left to Captain Marco to emancipate Raymond from the brainwashing he has been placed under, prevent the political assassination he's been programmed to commit, and save the American republic from Communist rule.

When *The Manchurian Candidate* first appeared in American cinemas, critics derided the film as farfetched. However, when President John F. Kennedy was assassinated in 1963, the movie's premise seemed to resonate with the conspiracy theories about Communist infiltration in American politics. As one scholar observes, "*The Manchurian Candidate* was thus transformed retrospectively from a wild and creative fantasy into a sober, although stylish, speculation." What made *The Manchurian Candidate* so powerful was the way in which the narrative arc of the film integrated contemporary anxieties about Communist infiltration with well-established racial anxieties—represented by the manipulative Dr. Yen Lo—about the "yellow peril" and manipulative "Orientals" conniving to get white Americans to perform murderous and treasonous acts that they would not ordinarily contemplate.[37]

Brownface in American Cinema

Hollywood's ability to integrate historical and contemporary racial and political anxieties into cinematic story lines also extended to Latinos, and especially Mexican Americans, throughout the twentieth century. D. W. Griffith made a significant contribution to presenting Latinos in a derogatory light in his early films. Griffith produced his first film in 1908; the same year he also produced *The Greaser's Gauntlet*. *The Greaser's Gauntlet* is a silent short film that incorporates one of the most offensive anti-Mexican epithets of the time. To contextualize the film's characterization of Mexicans as "greasers," the film revolves around an old west tale of robbery and drinking. Jose, portrayed by Wilfred Lewis in brownface, leaves old Mexico to make his way in the United States. While drinking in a saloon, he is soon framed for a robbery, actually committed by a Chinese character, the stereotypical thieving, wily Asian discussed earlier. In response, the saloon patrons call for the lynching of Jose. However, a lovely young woman discovers the Chinese character's duplicity and frees Jose. Years later, Jose is portrayed as a drunk, but, despite his insobriety, he is able to be cogent enough to save the same young woman from an attempted rape.

Griffith wove racial stereotypes into his films more effectively than any filmmaker of his era. He did this, as we discussed earlier, with *Birth of a Nation*, and he did it with films such as *The Greaser's Gauntlet* (1908), *The Vaquero's Vow* (1908), *The Red Man and the Child* (1908), or *The Thread of Destiny* (1910). Griffith was an equal opportunity racist, and as such, he portrayed black Sambos, Mexican bandits, Chinese thieves, and Native American savages in his many films. But early filmmakers were particularly obsessed with the term "greaser." That derogatory word appeared in the titles of numerous early silent films. Of these, *Tony, the Greaser* (1911); *The Greaser and the Weakling* (1912); *The Greaser's Revenge* (1914); *Broncho Billy and the Greaser* (1914 and 1915); *The Greaser* (1915); and *Guns and Greasers* (1918) are but a few. Of these, *The Greaser and the Weakling* and *Broncho Billy and the Greaser* merit further attention for the way they were representative of anti-Latino prejudices.

The Greaser and the Weakling (1912) uses family intrigue and a disputed inheritance to structure the film's plot. The movie focuses on the elderly Mrs. Burgess's death and her bequeathing her sprawling ranch to her daughters Mabel and Claudine. They are quickly caught up in a love triangle involving a ranch foreman named Johnny Williams, a man named Jim Bradley, and a duplicitous Mexican known only as "The Greaser," portrayed by Jack Richardson in brownface. The Greaser conspires with Bradley, the film's weakling who allows himself to be manipulated by The Greaser, convincing him that they should marry the women and gain title to the ranch. However, Johnny Williams eventually foils the plot with the assistance of another cowboy. *The Greaser and the Weakling* reiterates numerous anti-Mexican stereotypes of the early twentieth century. For instance, the film implies that Mexican men, like African American men, lusted after white women. In addition to representing Mexicans as sexual Lotharios, the film insinuates that they are thieves willing to cheat innocent people out of their property, a curious inversion of the land dispossession Mexican-origin people experienced throughout southwestern history.

Broncho Billy and the Greaser (1914) added to the growing cinematic archive of racist depictions of Mexican-descent people. In this film, "The Greaser" (Lee Willard) accosts a young woman, known only as "The Girl" (Marguerite Clayton), as she waits in line for the mail. The Greaser has a lustful, malicious look in his eyes, and she seems quite afraid of him. He even puts his hands on her, pushing and jostling her body. Broncho Billy (Gilbert M. Anderson) comes to The Girl's aid, forcing The Greaser out of the store at gunpoint. The Girl then focuses her affection on Broncho Billy.

The Greaser is enraged by this development. He begins drinking heavily, and when he sees Broncho Billy, he draws a knife (even though he has a six-shooter!) and ultimately takes Billy prisoner. The Girl musters her courage and follows The Greaser, enabling her to alert a group of white men of his whereabouts and misdeeds. They free Broncho Billy and remove The Greaser (presumably taking him away to be lynched, as routinely happened in the West and Southwest).[38] In the end, Billy gets The Girl.

Like many silent-era films, *The Greaser and the Weakling* and *Broncho Billy and the Greaser* relied on popular cultural clichés to propel the narrative of the films. Moreover, both movies relied on popular perceptions of "foreigners" as racial threats to the American body politic—a threat often represented by the sexual vulnerability of white women. In *Broncho Billy and the Greaser*, the eponymous The Greaser, again portrayed by a white actor in brownface, highlights this threat. In addition to the brownface character's contrived appearance demarcating foreignness and danger, The Greaser spends much of his time snarling at his opponent, drinking heavily, and handling various weapons in an overly dramatic fashion (a knife in one scene, a rope in another). The knife is especially relevant given that many Americans feared Mexican-origin people as "knife-wielding killers."[39] Willard's "greaser" prefers to wield a knife as his instrument of terror, but also carries a pistol. This choice of weapon differentiates The Greaser from his Anglo-American competitors, marking him as volatile, untrustworthy, violent, occasionally animal-like, and a thief. The Greaser is, in short, an example of the Mexican bandito, a character that came to be reviled in Hollywood films.

Building on the "greaser" archetype, filmmakers found great utility in the Mexican/Mexican American bandit character. Typically the bandit straddled the line between the criminal, antiestablishment "greaser" and the stereotypical "Latin lover." These representations occupied the spectrum of early twentieth-century racism in the United States toward Mexican people. Few characters better represent such stereotypical attributes than Zorro. From his debut in silent movies in the 1920s, Zorro has had a long career in Hollywood. Zorro first graced American movie screens in the 1920 film *The Mark of Zorro*. Douglas Fairbanks, who had a long career impersonating nonwhites (recall his Middle Eastern character "Ahmed" in the 1924 film *The Thief of Bagdad*), played Zorro. *The Mark of Zorro* had no fewer than 11 credited, Spanish-surnamed characters, none of whom were portrayed by Latino/Latina people (one character, "Bernardo," is played by Tote Du Crow, a Native American actor).

The Mark of Zorro provides audiences with Zorro's origins and lays out the story line that future Zorro movies would build on. Fairbanks's Zorro—unmasked he is Don Diego Vega—is a dandy, a somewhat effete elite who cares more about clothes than right or wrong. But upon seeing how the Spanish colonial regime mistreats local peasants, Don Diego becomes the swashbuckling Zorro. He rescues his love interest, Lolita Pulido (Marguerite De La Motte), from the evil Spanish governor, Alvarado (George Periolat), and turns the governor's troops into his own. Alvarado relinquishes his position and Zorro wins the day.

While Zorro represents a silver screen hero, he is a hero who fits into the stereotypical viewpoints that Hollywood, and many Americans, had about Latinos. In this case he is a thinly disguised bandito, a Robin Hood–like character. More importantly, he is a Latin lover who fights for his woman and wins the day, and the heart of the woman he desires. In contrast, the other Latinos portrayed in *The Mark of Zorro* are ignoble, drunken fools who abuse their power and authority and lack moral decency. Thus, while we may find some minor positive attributes in the Zorro character, those attributes are set against a broader cultural context in which more villainous Latinos portrayed by whites in brownface are the norm.

The Zorro character was originally based in part on the exploits of Joaquin Murrieta, a Californio man from Sonora, Mexico, who participated in the1849 Gold Rush only to have his claim taken by jealous Anglo miners. Those Anglo miners allegedly gang raped his wife and killed his brother. Murrieta retaliated by becoming a bandit, the havoc he caused leading to white people despising him.[40] The underpinnings of Murrieta's tale was evidently lost on the creators of the Zorro story, who, in *The Mark of Zorro* and subsequent Zorro films, preferred to see Zorro as a swashbuckling hero who stood up to corrupt Spanish officials as opposed to a viciously wronged Mexican who stood up to Americans.

As in the Zorro films, very similar elements pervade the Cisco Kid. The original Cisco movie, *The Caballero's Way*, loosely follows the novel of the same title by O. Henry in 1907. In O. Henry's telling, the Cisco Kid is a ruthless outlaw who kills for sport and does not appear to be of Mexican extraction. In the film versions, however, the Cisco Kid is a Mexican bandit, almost always played by white actors, who like Zorro has certain noble qualities—he is Robin Hood–like and does not kill. But most of the other Mexicans who appear in the film are portrayed negatively.

In Old Arizona (1929), the first talkie to feature Cisco Kid movie, the stereotypical racial attributes define the Cisco Kid's representation. The Cisco

Kid, played by white actor Warner Baxter, is a kind-hearted, yet equally buffoonish, Western hero who steals in order to buy gifts for his love, Tonia. He is, as such, a male version of the Latin lover. Tonia, played by Dorothy Burgess, is the female version of the Latin lover, the overtly sexual (and sexualized) Latina. However, Tonia is also duplicitous, taking the Cisco Kid's gifts while she cheats on him with another man. She eventually falls in with the local law enforcer, Dunn, and together they concoct a plan to capture or kill the Kid, turn him over to authorities, and share the reward money. The Kid gets wise to these plans and tricks Tonia and Dunn by writing a note in Tonia's handwriting stating that the Cisco Kid will attempt to flee Tonia's home in disguise, wearing Tonia's clothes. When Dunn sees a figure in the clothes mentioned in the note, he shoots, killing not the Cisco Kid, but Tonia. The Cisco Kid then escapes.[41]

As with many major motion pictures that used the Southwest and Mexican-origin people as a backdrop, *In Old Arizona* featured white performers in brownface.

The addition of sound helped to magnify the discriminatory elements in *In Old Arizona*. Both the Kid and Tonia speak in an overly accented way, using broken English that was meant to demarcate authentic "Mexican-ness" to American audiences. Tonia, in one of her scenes with Dunn, for instance, is being taught to sing the song "The Bowery." She pronounces it "the browrie," the "brar-rie," and "the bar-rie." Baxter's Cisco Kid frequently drops his Mexican-like accent but also speaks using broken English. In a scene with Tonia, for instance, he says, "Ah Tonia, bebia ... de touch of jur hand is like de touch of an angel." Along with their speaking style, both Baxter and Burgess are stereotypically dressed and both have their faces slightly darkened to appear more authentically Mexican. Neither, however, actually looks Hispanic—they look like white people pretending to be brown. That doesn't really matter, though, for at this time and for many years later American audiences found white actors who portrayed ethnic "others" to be more authentic than actors from ethnic communities. Baxter's performance was evidently so authentic that he won the Academy Award for Best Actor for his portrayal of the Cisco Kid. Baxter reprised his role in several other films, and numerous other Cisco Kid movies were made, almost all starring white actors except for several in the 1930s and 1940s starring Cuban American actor Cesar Romero.[42]

As Burgess made clear for Tonia, Latinas either were not depicted in major motion pictures or were depicted as highly sexualized objects of male desire, the proverbial Latina lover, or, to borrow a title from numerous films, a "Mexican Spitfire."[43] Take, for instance, the 1940 hit *Mexican Spitfire*. That film was a sequel to the more innocuously titled *The Girl from Mexico* (1939). A half dozen other Mexican Spitfire films appeared in the 1940s. These films differed ever so slightly from films featuring the Cisco Kid in that the star character, the Mexican Spitfire, was portrayed by Mexican actress Lupe Velez. *Mexican Spitfire* dealt with some important themes, including interethnic marriage. In general, the film relied on well-worn clichés about highly sexualized Latinas. The film revolved around the marriage of two performers, Dennis Lindsay (Donald Wood) and Carmelita Lindsay (Velez), he white, she Mexican American. One of the obstacles they must overcome is her seemingly fiery demeanor. More importantly, there is a duplicitous ex-fiancé who seeks nothing more than to break up the marriage. Presented as a comedy, the film falls flat because of its reliance on overly determined racialized caricatures.

Other Latinas found themselves similarly typecast. Alongside the Mexican Spitfire, for example, there existed the "Cuban Fireball."[44] While the

Cuban Fireball character was almost always a woman, a male version of this character type could also be viewed, perhaps most famously in the guise of Ricky Ricardo of *I Love Lucy* (1951, 1953) fame and later Tony Montana in *Scarface* (1983). But in the first half of the twentieth century, the Cuban Fireball was usually a female character. Good examples of this stereotypical character can be found in films such as *Cuban Fireball* (1951) and *Tropical Heat Wave* (1952). Both of these films starred Estelita Rodriguez, the eponymous Cuban Fireball—or "fiery Señorita"—of the late 1940s and early 1950s.[45] In these films, Rodriguez plays a recent Cuban immigrant to the United States, is usually an entertainer of some sort, is highly sexualized, but winds up in trouble and in need of rescue by a white American benefactor.

In *Cuban Fireball*, Rodriguez plays a stereotypical version of a female gold digger named Estelita. At the start of the film she is employed as an entertainer in a *tabaquero*, a Cuban cigar-making factory. One of her routines has her mocking her employer, and she nearly gets fired for affronting him. But when she learns that she's inherited a number of oil wells in Los Angeles, to the tune of $20,000,000, all is quickly forgiven and she is LA bound. In order to discourage similar attention, she disguises herself as an ugly woman. This disguise does not seem to work—her innate, exotic beauty shines through and Tommy, the son of the current manager of the petroleum company, soon falls in love with Estelita. The film devolves into a series of slapstick moments as Estelita, playing two different women, finds herself involved in a string of mishaps, the most serious of which is when an LA gangster discovers her windfall and kidnaps Estelita. Tommy comes to her rescue, an act that wins her heart.

Tropical Heat Wave follows a similar narrative arc as *Cuban Fireball*. Rodriguez again plays the "fiery Señorita." This time, Estelita is an immigrant from Cuba who settles in New York City. A former night club performer in Cuba, she soon finds work singing at her uncle's Manhattan nightclub. There Estelita meets Norman, a notorious gangster who threatens her with violence unless she helps him take control of the night club. A local criminology professor, Stratford Carver, befriends Estelita. He comes to her aid by posing as an even more dangerous hoodlum in an attempt to scare Norman away. This ploy, while ham-handed, ultimately works and Stratford and Estelita live happily ever after.

These Cuban Fireball films were formulaic in their plot structure: a recent émigré arrives in America; finds wealth, fame, or fortune; encounters a bad guy; and is rescued by a noble white benefactor. The ethno-racial and gendered messages illuminate the patriarchal nature of American racial hierarchies during the early twentieth century. As in other depictions of the period, Latinas are portrayed as hypersexual temptresses who seem to delight in carnal pleasure. Estelita, both the character and the actress, conforms to this mold. Her representation of the "fiery Señorita" delights an almost exclusively white, male audience. Her thick accent and exoticness mark Estelita as a sexually accessible ethnic "other," both racializing and sexualizing her simultaneously.

Given this historical context, it is not surprising that Estelita Rodriguez, like other Latino/Latina actors of the period, found herself typecast. She began her career, for instance, portraying Mexican border women in Westerns such as *Along the Navajo Trail* (1947) and *Old Los Angeles* (1948). Rodriguez came to dislike these types of roles, so she left Hollywood, only to return to portray equally one-dimensional Cuban Fireball roles. Numerous other actors found similar limitations in Hollywood, such as Rita Moreno, Carmen Miranda, Rita Hayworth (a.k.a. Margarita Cansino), and the aforementioned Anna May Wong. Moreno, commenting on the problem of Latina typecasting, spoke for many of her contemporaries when she quipped: "Latinas. You know the kind I mean—spitfires, girls with wild tempers."[46]

While Cuban- and Mexican-origin women found themselves typecast as "fireballs" or "spitfires," Puerto Rican actors—male and female—found themselves portraying urban delinquents. Or to put it in a slightly different way, Puerto Ricans were portrayed as urban delinquents by white actors, since many European Americans played the prominent roles depicting Puerto Ricans. Such was the case with the most famous film to "portray" Puerto Ricans: *West Side Story* (1961). As scholar Frances Negron-Muntaner observes, "There is no single American cultural product that haunts Puerto Rican identity discourses in the United States more intensely than the 1961 film, *West Side Story.* "[47] In many ways, that film depicts Puerto Ricans as urban *bandidos*, latter-day versions of the criminal bandits of Westerns discussed earlier. And the type of banditry represented in *West Side Story* was often labeled similarly to the Westerns, with offenders being the proverbial "greasers."

West Side Story follows many of the well-established Hollywood stereotypes of Latinos/Latinas. For instance, one of the principal characters, Maria Nuñez, is portrayed by star Natalie Wood in a classic brownface depiction. Meanwhile, the supporting character of Anita del Carmen, Maria's friend and sidekick, is played by Puerto Rican actress Rita Morena. Thus, a white actress plays the main role in a film about Puerto Ricans, while the actual Puerto Rican star appeared as a minor character. As in numerous other films, the lead male role of Bernardo Nuñez went to a white star, Greek American actor George Chakiris, whose swarthy looks perhaps made him seem Puerto Rican. Almost all of the other ethnic roles in the film went to white, non-Latino stars. Makeup artists lightly darkened Natalie Wood's skin, thereby bringing the brownface tradition into the latter half of the twentieth century.

The narrative of *West Side Story* also raises questions about Hollywood's treatment of race and ethnicity. As numerous reviewers quickly discerned, *West Side Story* is a modern retelling of *Romeo and Juliet*, a love story that had much to say about perceptions of difference. In *West Side Story*, however, the sophisticated way in which Shakespeare used *Romeo and Juliet* to address issues of family and differences in social status was lost, replaced by a fairly cheap, tawdry exploration of elicit interethnic sexual relations. The movie fixates on the gang rivalry shared by the Jets, a group of local white toughs, and the Sharks, a Puerto Rican gang. The two gangs have a series of "rumbles," at which point the leader of the Jets, Tony, meets Maria. The two fall in love. Alas, Bernardo, the leader of the Sharks and Maria's brother, will never allow his sister to be with a Jet. From this point forward the two gangs battle to prevent this relationship from blossoming. During one of these fights, Tony kills Bernardo, but Maria—the hot-blooded Latina—professes her continued love for Tony. In the end, one of Bernardo's friends kills Tony, and the film concludes with Maria attempting to stop the gang violence as Bernardo's funeral commences.

West Side Story was a box office smash and many Americans remember it fondly. It is, however, a film filled with racial and ethnic stereotypes. The foreignness of the Puerto Rican characters is accentuated, as the film taps into the motif of "immigrants," as opposed to the New Yorkers that they actually are, trying to make it in America. Compounding the affect of foreignness, the Puerto Rican characters speak (and sing) with thick accents and broken English. During the famous "America" song, for example, that word is spoken in an overly emphatic way. The chorus section of that song features the line "Ev'rything free in America" (not "everything's free"). One female star sings "Industry boom in America." That kind of spoken "dialect," the overly trilled "R" or the dropped "S," to the producer's and director's way of thinking, probably made the actors sound authentically Puerto Rican. Certainly some Puerto Ricans have accents. Just as surely, though, Puerto Ricans have one of the highest percentages of English speakers in the Latin

American world, and many Puerto Ricans in places like New York are not immigrants but native-born Americans. In other words, Puerto Ricans sound like other Americans.

In addition to representing Puerto Ricans in these stereotypical ways, *West Side Story* depicts Puerto Rican people in gender-specific ways. Women, for example, are represented as sex objects, while men are portrayed as ready-to-knife-you gangbangers. As such, just about every cultural stereotype about Latinos appears in this film (and theatrical versions on Broadway). Building on stereotypes and clichés in operation since Hollywood films began portraying Latinos/Latinas in the early twentieth century, *West Side Story* depicts criminality, the use of knives, the hypersexuality of the women, the gangs, and the laziness assumed to be character traits (or flaws) of Latinos/Latinas.

Stereotypical depictions of Latinos continued after *West Side Story*. The use of well-established racial and gender tropes reflected broader societal concerns about racialized groups of immigrants entering the United States. *West Side Story* emerged at a time when juvenile delinquency was a hot topic, especially as it pertained to ethnic communities. These themes ran through similar films, such as *The Young Savages* (1961) and *Fort Apache, the Bronx* (1981). Other films focused on other hot-button issues. *Scarface* (1983), while ostensibly a classic retelling of the 1932 gangster flick of the same title, was also about American discomfort with the Cuban Mariel boatlift and the (fictitious) flood of criminals released from Castro's prisons.[48] *American Me* (1992) dealt with similar issues as they pertained to the Mexican American community. While Hollywood has become more sophisticated with how it represents the Latino community, as the sympathetic portrayals of Latinos in films such as *El Norte* (1983) or *Spanglish* (2004) suggest, there are still performances—such as *The Mexican* (2001)— that repeat brownface representations of yesteryear.

Native Americans in American Cinema

For Native Americans, moviemakers tended to fixate on the great horse cultures of the Plains and American Southwest. Groups such as the Apache, the Comanche, the Sioux, and the Navajo provided ample, and highly fictional, fodder for producers and directors. Of course, prominent indigenous people, from Geronimo to Cochise to Sitting Bull, were often featured in major films. But just as often, Hollywood focused on tribes as a whole, reducing native peoples to nothing more than a group of marauding individuals with little discernable structure or leadership. These are films made by white people, for white audiences, and often feature white actors in leading redface roles. They present native people as frozen in time in fairly standard "cowboys and Indians" or army and Native American movies.

Silent-era films explored a number of themes salient to indigenous peoples. Among the more popular films were movies of quiet desperation, such as *An Eye for an Eye* (1909) in which the wife leaves her husband for a younger man. Alternatively, films like *The Blight of Sin* (1909) delved into the impact that a husband's excessive gambling had on his wife, who turns to another man for companionship. Alcoholism also features in silent-era films. For example, *The Iconoclast* (1910) emphasizes how the occasional tipple resulted in one man becoming an alcoholic, something that caused significant stress in his family.

Silent-era films about Native Americans also joined this list of popular genres. While the only silent movie known to have been performed by Native Americans was *The Daughters of Dawn* (1920), silent films depicting Native Americans typically used white actors in redface to portray indigenous characters. This was the case with D. W. Griffith's films like *Comata, the Sioux* (1909), a short film about a Native American woman who falls in love with a cowboy; *The Chief's Daughter* (1911), the story of a white man who wants to marry the daughter of a Native American chief; and *The Battle at Elderbrush Gulch* (1913), a story of frontier life and the ever-present danger of Native American violence.

These short films did not exceed 30 minutes in duration and were simplistic in plot. However, increasingly sophisticated story lines were being developed, albeit in racially clichéd ways. One of the best examples of Hollywood's negative portrayals of the Apache can be found in 1939's *Stagecoach*. That movie involves an assortment of strangers who are traveling across Arizona. The Apaches in the film, led by Geronimo, are largely unseen savages on the warpath. They are represented at various moments as little more than an ominous threat—a smoke signal here, a one-word telegraph with the name "Geronimo" there. Only near the end of the film do the Apache appear. They attack the stagecoach, with loud war cries and Native Americans–sounding music. Carrying both guns and spears, the Apache surround the stagecoach but are also picked off by Ringo Kid (John Wayne) and his accomplices. Almost out of ammunition, the Native Americans will surely kill the white folks on the stagecoach. But at the last minute the Cavalry arrives and saves the day. The Apaches then recede from the film, disappearing back into the desert somewhere, no longer a nuisance to civilization.

Stagecoach in many ways became a model for cowboys and Native Americans film. Its use of a mainly nameless, faceless horde of fierce warrior savages confirmed for many Americans what the Old West, and indigenous people, were really like. They were destined to challenge the progress of civilization—never to stop it—and then to recede from view. They were bloodthirsty and always looking to exact revenge, although the reasons for that revenge seeking often remained unclear. A similar story arc can be found in numerous other films of the period, most notably *Rio Grande* (1950) and the aptly titled *Fort Massacre* (1958).

While *Stagecoach* and other similar films focused on a nameless, disappearing group of Native Americans, other films of this era tended to focus on assimilation and cross-racial contact. These films often included both fierce warrior and noble savage motifs. For instance, *The Last Wagon* (1956) featured a primary character, Comanche Todd, who had lived with the Native Americans for many years. Similarly, in *Arrowhead* Jack Palance offers a redface portrayal of Toriano, a bloodthirsty Native American who is juxtaposed in the film against his white brother. Toriano has assimilated into white society, but uncomfortably so. He eventually kills his brother before being killed by a white army officer, Bannon played by Charlton Heston. The role of the white Indian, the go-between for the indigenous and white worlds, was perhaps most evident in Westerns such as *Little Big Man* (1970) and *A Man Called Horse* (1970). Unlike *Arrowhead*, those two films portray white Indians, and Native Americans more generally, in a sympathetic light.

What are more rare, however, are films wherein the fierce warrior and noble savage are, in essence, the same character, played by the same actor. No film better illustrates this type of motion picture than the 1968 paella Western (because it was filmed in Spain) *The White Comanche*. This movie is also interesting in that it is a more modern version of classic redface given that the titular "white Comanche" is played by Canadian-born actor William Shatner of *Star Trek* fame. Shatner plays a dual role as both Johnny Moon, an outcast drifter of Comanche ancestry who has attempted to assimilate into American society, and Notah, Moon's twin brother, who is the leader of a group of Comanche. The film is filled with ugly moments, crass racial and sexist stereotypes, and a convoluted and hackneyed plot.

The White Comanche opens with Moon barely escaping a lynch mob. He is, evidently, frequently confused as his twin brother, who routinely attacks white settlers. Moon escapes this attempted lynching and travels to Notah's village to confront his twin about this mistaken identity. The action shifts to a stagecoach and Notah lying in wait; a shirtless Shatner with a headband/ bandana, brown pants, nearly knee high moccasin boots, and war paint on his face appears on camera. He performs an odd-sounding "ay yay yay yay" war cry before attacking the coach with a group of Native American followers. All the white men on the coach are killed before Notah notices a young white woman in the stagecoach; he notes her not by sight but by the smell of her perfume. He chases her down, chokes her, slaps her about with an evil-looking grimace, before the scene ends, leaving the impression that he will rape this young woman. The initial confrontation between Johnny and Notah occurs shortly thereafter when the war party returns to the village. Interestingly, Notah is assisted by a pregnant wife, or "squaw," as she is later called. Johnny, in his own clearly "native" speaking pattern, says, "Notah is well named. His liver is white like his Yankee father. His heart burns blacker than the skin of his Comanche mother. He's white belly, like his name, a snake." Notah responds in kind, saying, "Notah's brother talks like the white man he thinks he is. He's afraid to be Comanche." Notah then consumes peyote while Johnny castigates him for continuing the "war path" while times have surely changed. The two agree to have a dual to the death at Rio Hondo in four days.

Johnny Moon travels to Rio Hondo at about the same time the stagecoach robbed by Notah has arrived. The woman we now learn is named Kelly and has clearly been raped, but her traumatic experience is quickly passed over. She sees Johnny and assumes he is Notah and attempts to shoot him. She later confronts Johnny in his hotel room, but learns that Johnny was not the individual who raped her (because Johnny and Notah have different colored eyes, you see). Kelly befriends Johnny, convinced of his innocence, and they eventually fall in love. Meanwhile, Notah prepares for battle with Johnny by getting high on peyote and communicating with heaven. Many of his followers have grown wary of his machinations, so Notah leaves to fight Johnny Moon alone. Their final confrontation is laughable. Comanche dueling techniques are portrayed as involving opponents riding toward each other on horseback while shooting, a kind of latter-day joust. Johnny wins the day. He then leads the Comanche back to the reservation.

While one could argue that there are feminist and nationalist critiques with *The White Comanche*—Kelly attempts to punish her attacker, albeit confusing Johnny and Notah; Johnny declares at one point Notah's feud against white people: "It's been like this a long time, ever since the Comanches were forced onto the reservation in Oklahoma … came across some soldiers one day and they forced us onto the reservation"—such an argument would strain the importance of the film. It is incredibly violent for its time, with men being shot in the forehead, Notah's pregnant wife getting stabbed to death, a man being trampled by a horse, and more. But it is the racist imagery we are concerned with, and *The White Comanche* contains much of this. As in many other forms of popular media, the main "Indians" in this film are all played by white actors. This is classic redface, and since they most likely cannot speak Comanche they instead speak with guttural grunts or with a Native American–sounding dialect. The Native Americans in the film are therefore not only inaccurate but also inauthentic, fictitious creations of Hollywood writers who think grunts and war cries and fake Native American dueling/jousting competitions seem "Indian" and real.

Most importantly, the Johnny Moon/Notah characters represent the bipolar stereotypical portrayal of indigenous people. On the one hand, Johnny is in many ways the noble savage, a Native American who stands for right and defends the innocent. He has recognized the benefits of the white world, even if he fits uncomfortably into that world. Notah, on the other hand, is the fierce Native American warrior. He longs for battle and has sworn to make war on white people—any white people—as revenge for past wrongs. He robs, rapes, fights, and kills. Interestingly, he can also be viewed as the classic drunken Native American, since he partakes of peyote, becomes inebriated, and has visions of grandeur that include killing whites and creating a Comanche nation. The moral of Johnny and Notah is that each is the other. This film is a classic me-against-myself type depiction, in this case literally so. The two are frequently referred to as "half breeds," which provides a further message in the film: interracial sex is ultimately destructive because it leads to the creation of monstrously barbarous people like Notah. In the end, the civilized, noble savage—Johnny Moon—emerges victorious and leads the Native Americans back to the reservation, where they can have peace but just as assuredly be separated and contained from decent society.

Conclusion

The films we have analyzed in this chapter reflect the broad spectrum of cinematic representations of racialized groups in twentieth-century America. Our analysis is not intended to be exhaustive, but is instead designed to highlight the evolving role played by the motion picture industry in reinforcing social and cultural ideas about race, in broadcasting such ideas to massive audiences, and in institutionalizing racism in the American popular media. Film has played, and continues to play, a dual role in shaping race and racism in American society: it holds up a mirror to societal prejudices, while simultaneously helping give shape and meaning to expressions of racism. For these reasons, we hope that our analysis will encourage readers to view movies as more than entertainment and to view film in a more critical light that allows us to see the depth of cinema's impact on American society. Just as Americans have learned not to passively internalize the messages contained in advertising, so film should be viewed as a two-way lens in which filmmakers mirror societal attitudes and behaviors, and audiences are informed by, and conscious of the need to critique, the messages contained in Hollywood movies. This proved a difficult task for most twentieth-century adults who were exposed to racism in motion pictures, just as their children were exposed to the racist cartoon industry, the subject of Chapter 4.

Chapter 4

Animating Racism

In February 1940, cartoon gurus William Hanna and Joseph Barbera introduced one of the most famous duos in animation history. In "Puss Gets the Boot," the world met Tom Cat and Jerry Mouse for the first time.[1] Known as Jasper and Jinx in the premiere episode, generations of children subsequently grew to know these characters as Tom and Jerry. The *Tom and Jerry* series became a national, and global, phenomenon, with hundreds of shorts, myriad series spinoffs, and nearly a dozen full-length feature films produced in the half century after its premiere. In that very first short in 1940, audiences also saw for the first time an unnamed character. She was a large, dark-skinned black woman who spoke in a vernacular dialect that was overlaid with a thick southern accent. That unnamed character also wore brightly colored clothing and was usually only visible from the waist down. This unnamed character became known as "Mammy Two Shoes," a "galumphing black domestic."[2] Mammy Two Shoes was typically seen only from the waist down, was buffoonish in nature, and was, in essence, an animated version of a black-blackface representation of the popular Mammy archetype.[3]

It has become cliché to note that the "golden age" of cartoon production between the 1920s and late 1960s, so characterized because of the addition of sound to animation, also produced the most racist and sexist depictions of people of color in cartoon history. Mammy Two Shoes was a product of this golden age. She was joined by a host of other racialized and racist characters, some of whom existed during the silent era and received new life with the advent of sound. Cartoonists, their production companies and studios, and the prominent directors and producers between the 1920s and 1960s brought their racial–ethnic biases to their animated creations, in addition to mirroring societal attitudes and cultural assumptions about race. Prominent figures in the world of animation, such as William Hanna and Joseph Barbera, Otto Messmer, Max Fleischer, Walt Disney, Friz Freleng, and Tex Avery, created cartoons that portrayed communities of color not only in stereotypical ways but in a negative and racist light.[4] Such depictions did not simply constitute harmless forms of children's entertainment; rather, the cartoons that these men helped to create and popularize became part of a racist understanding of American society and culture in which racism became a casually accepted and internalized part of a person's life from a very young age.[5]

Cartoons frequently portrayed explicit forms of racism, utilizing stock motifs and images such as the lazy Latino, the cannibalistic native, the rotund and dutiful Mammy, and the wily "Oriental." From the silent era to the early years of animation's golden age, cartoons produced for either adults or children both reaffirmed and taught American audiences how to think and speak about race. Significantly, animation has from its earliest years targeted children, making the racist messages and representations in cartoons a critical component of a child's socialization into U.S. racial culture. Through characters like Felix the Cat, Mickey Mouse, Speedy Gonzalez, and Tom and Jerry, American children learned about race in the United States. This exposure to racialized language and images was all the more powerful given the seemingly innocent ways in which cartoons reinforced racism as a normative aspect of American cultural life during the twentieth century.

In this chapter we take a closer look at how popular forms of animation communicated racism to American audiences. In so doing, we demonstrate how racist cartoons became a didactic form of entertainment that taught viewers, particularly children, about racial "others." The humor and slapstick antics of cartoon characters thus masked the racism that became institutionalized in the animation industry during the twentieth century. Moreover, the racism woven into the story lines of cartoons prepared children for adult life and provided them with a vocabulary and understanding of the different forms of racism embedded in American writing, cinema, and advertising. To highlight these cultural processes, we begin this chapter by examining the racism prevalent during the silent era of cartoon production, transition to animation during the early golden age of cartoons, and conclude with an overview of mid- and late twentieth-century cartoons—some of which were banned by American censors—that exposed viewers to different forms of racism at a young age.

Animated Racism in the Silent Era and Early Golden Age

Racist or stereotypical depictions of people of color go back to the silent era of American cartoon production between the 1910s and the 1930s. Early cartoon production relied on hand drawing and rotoscoping (animation traced using live-action footage), techniques that meant early black and white cartoon depictions lent themselves to the production of blackface characters. For these reasons, early cartoons often featured black-and-white anthropomorphic animals, such as Felix the Cat and Mickey Mouse. Cultural critic Jeet Heer recently observed the racialized qualities imposed on many of these cartoon characters, explaining that "Felix the cat is a feckless, happy-go-lucky trickster. Culturally, he's the missing link between Br'er Rabbit and Bugs Bunny: admirable in some ways but lacking in the 'white' qualities of respectability and responsibility."[6] Heer's analysis reminds us of how animated characters like Felix and Mickey represented animalistic blackface depictions, their coloration conveniently approximating blackface performers such as Al Jolson's *Jazz Singer*. Political scientist Michael Rogin has made a similar observation, arguing that "the most ubiquitous cartoon character of all, Walt Disney's white-gloved and black-faced Mickey Mouse, was copied from the *Jazz Singer*."[7] Indeed, the creators of animated characters were quite explicit in acknowledging the racial inspiration for their creations. For example, Otto Messmer, the creator of Felix the Cat, stated that this character "was a pickaninny."[8] Other popular silent-era cartoons, such as *The Alice Comedies*, featured a black and white cat, Julius, while *Koko the Clown* featured a black and white human clown, cleverly approximated blackface minstrel performers.

Otto Messmer's Felix the Cat was arguably the first animated powerhouse of the silent era. The inaugural Felix episodes were fairly innocuous. But in "Felix Saves the Day" (1922) we see many of the common racist stereotypes of the day, including the pickaninny and an interracial baseball game. The short begins with a depiction of the "Tar Heels," a black baseball team whose members are all black-blackface pickaninnies.[9] Felix and his friend Willie practice their game so that they can beat the Tar Heels. In one scene, Felix bats a ball that hits a police officer and lands in the mouth of another blackface individual, who appears to be a trash collector. Willie ends up in jail for Felix's transgression against the police officer. While in jail, the Tar Heels begin to easily defeat Willie's team, the "Nifty Nine." Felix, however, saves the day. Critical to this early cartoon was the cultural understandings about race and racism that it conveyed. The black characters featured in the episode represented white perceptions of black inferiority, complete with nappy hair, bright white eyes and lips, and long apelike arms.[10]

In other Felix episodes, black characters provide comic relief, much like the blackface trash collector who swallows Willie's ball. In "Tee Time," for example, Felix's antics result in the fire department being called out to a golf course. They spray Felix with a fire hose, the force of which is enough to knock him out into an ocean and eventually to an island. While tom-tom drums bang, a group of monkey-like black, "cannibal," "savage" islanders chase after Felix. He hides in a tree and uses coconuts to hammer one black islander into the sand. Like other silent-era shorts, "Tee Time" presented the supposed savagery of African-looking peoples in a particularly violent manner, lampooning their twentieth-century American counterparts in the process.

Such depictions of Felix the Cat continued into the early golden age of animation. One short, "The Non-Stop Fright" (1927) featured Felix participating in a flying contest. As in "Tee Time" Felix encountered a group of "cannibal" black natives. The "cannibals" chase Felix, all the while shouting an undecipherable "native" gibberish. Felix escapes this mob, although one of the blacks continues to yell at him. "The Non-Stop Fright" made explicit how the islanders were meant to not only appear as savage cannibals but also sound like racialized savages.

By the late 1920s, Felix episodes had begun to caricature other people of color. In 1929, for instance, the short "False Vases" mocked Asian people. The episode opened with stereotypical Asian-sounding music. As the music plays, Felix breaks a lamp and goes to a merchant to buy a new one. The merchant, a stereotypically depicted Chinese individual with narrowly drawn epicanthic fold "slanted" eyes, long robes, and an evil grin, attempts to cheat Felix. This Chinese individual also speaks in an odd Chinese-sounding gibberish. This encounter results in Felix traveling to China to replace the vase, where he encounters numerous similarly caricatured Chinese people. The episode was thus a good example of "yellowface."

In numerous ways, Felix the Cat set the stage for later racist animation. As the first cartoon superstar whose fame extended from the silent era to the golden era, Felix undoubtedly touched many generations of Americans. While later cartoons, such as Tom and Jerry, offered the public riffs on common ethnic stereotypes, especially the Mammy archetype via Mammy Two Shoes, Felix the Cat's stereotypes were more basic and limited. In many of the early episodes, the silent quality of the cartoon reduced the presence of people of color to more limited visual portrayals of buffoonary and savagery. In later golden age sound cartoons, the "natives" and Asians whom Felix encountered were accompanied by stereotypical background music and racialized dialect that amounted to little more than undecipherable gibberish. These aural qualities magnified the racial caricature at work. If, for instance, the black trash collector in "Tee Time," who appeared as the stereotypical pickaninny, spoke with a sophisticated English accent, the foreignness of his racial representation may well have been significantly diluted.

One of the most prolific and influential cartoonists to use racialized imagery was Walt Disney. While Mickey Mouse remains Disney's best-known creation, his first cartoon, *The Alice Comedies*, foreshadowed how Disney would incorporate racial depictions into his subsequent creations. These shorts combined live-action scenes and real people with animation. Alice, a live-action little girl played Virginia Davis (1923–1925, 1926), Margie Gay (1926–1927), and Louis Hardwick (1927), routinely interacted with the cartoon cat, Julius. In the first short, "Alice's Wonderland" (1923), Alice asks to see how cartoons are created. In response, an animator takes her on a tour of his production studio. The first thing Alice sees on this tour is a group of blackface cats playing jazz. Later, when she goes to sleep, Alice dreams of riding an animated train into Julius's animated world. Upon her arrival, a monkey porter helps her from the train. Considering numerous black men worked as porters, the cartoon monkey porter was designed to reinforce the popular notion that black people typically worked in jobs that served white people. The denizens of the animated city subsequently welcome Alice with a parade, during which a number of blackface characters appear.

In the 1926 short "Alice's Mysterious Mysteries," a dog-catcher and his mouse comrade dress in Ku Klux Klan robes to catch dogs at a dog training school for the purpose of turning them into sausage. However, Alice and Julius save the day, defeating these "Klansmen." The Klan is portrayed negatively in this short, a stark contrast from the Klan's positive depiction in an earlier short, "Alice and the Dog Catcher" (1924). In that short, Alice presides over a group called the "Secret Klub of the Kook Klaks" (sometimes referred to as the "Klix Klax Klub"). Alice's KKK, reminiscent of the Little Rascals, is composed of children who wear brown paper bags, instead of white robes, as their hoods. Those bags/hoods have humorous faces drawn on them. One of the children wearing a bag is an African American boy with a blackface face drawn on his paper bag. In these outfits, the children help stop live-action dog-catchers from capturing their canine friend and KKK mascot. Upon initial examination, the depictions of the Klan seem comically odd. However, the KKK's reemergence in the 1920s was no laughing matter. As the paramount militant and racist organization in the United States, the Klan symbolized the most virulent form of white supremacist racism of its era. Therefore, even when the group was depicted negatively, as was the case with the sausage-making dog-catchers, the racist connotations associated with those representations penetrate through the cartoon humor. Moreover, the presence of the black child KKK member is also telling. When he doffs his blackface bag, the child's expression appears as one of befuddlement, an expression that was broken by a smirk that appears on his face, a hint to the viewer that he was too stupid to understand the kind of group he had joined.

Alice's world was a place defined by racism. Numerous other Alice cartoons emphasized this point. In "Alice's Wild West Show" (1924), for example, her Klan friends stage a series of Western skits. In these skits, the one black member of the group performed only menial tasks; he cleans up a saloon in one scene, while in another he stands with a confused look on his face as he holds a sign (upside down) indicating the first act will begin. Once Alice gets into the cartoon world she is on a stagecoach pursued by several Native Americans on horseback. In stereotypical "cowboys and Indians" fashion, Alice shoots the Native Americans off their horses.[11]

Alice encounters other ethnic groups in equally stereotypical ways. In "Alice Chops the Suey" (1925), Alice and Julius enter "Chinatown," with stereotypical Asian music playing in the background. Alice and her companion encounter several Chinese-looking characters, who, on spotting Alice, take her prisoner. These characters conformed to all of the anti-Asian caricatures of the era: sharpened teeth, "slanted" eyes, and long queues. They also speak in stereotypical "Oriental" dialect. This format was repeated in scores of other Alice shorts. In "Alice Cans the Cannibals" (1925), Alice and Julius find themselves on an island. There, they encounter a group of ape-like, blackface cannibals who throw spears at Alice and Julius. These cannibals also perform an odd dance and make unintelligible noises. In one of the final scenes, Alice throws a harpoon attached to a rope in the direction of the blackface characters. The harpoon pierces the large lips of four of the cannibals before striking a hippopotamus, which then drags the four cannibals—by their lips—into a lake.[12]

Numerous other instances of cartoon racism make their appearance in *The Alice Comedies*.[13] As one of the premier cartoons, like *Felix the Cat*, to transcend the silent era and thrive into the golden era of cartoons, these shorts set the stage for later cartoons. In these cartoons, Disney recycled many of the racist ideas and themes of previous Alice cartoons. For example, when Julius speaks in later episodes he sounds much like Mickey Mouse. Also, the use of animated and live-action characters persisted well into the golden age, a technique that in fact continues today. But it was the caricaturing of people of color that served as the most enduring aspect of these shorts. Certainly the black and white coloration of the series lent itself to blackface imagery. But the depictions of other ethnic groups, including the addition of stereotypical dialects and music, fit into the broader cultural imagery of white Americans and nonwhite others.[14]

Disney followed *The Alice Comedies* with *Oswald the Lucky Rabbit* and *Mickey Mouse*. While Oswald became a popular character, it was Mickey that emerged as a fixture at Disney. Many of the shorts in the *Mickey Mouse* series contained the same racist material used in other cartoons of the silent era to early golden age period. For instance, Mickey's nemesis Pete, who also appeared in *The Alice Comedies* and *Oswald*, was first referred to as "Black Pete." He was originally a burly, dark-haired bear, whose facial features approximated blackface caricatures. Only in later episodes was his appearance softened into the form of a large cat, and he became simply "Pete." Like Felix the Cat, Mickey Mouse is a black and white faced character whose own appearance evinced the broad outlines of stereotypical blackface characters. Indeed, many *Mickey Mouse* shorts feature a visual joke involving a momentary shot of a character in blackface. In "Gulliver Mickey" (1934), for instance, two Lilliputians fight over a fountain pen. When the pen shoots its ink, one of the Lilliputians appears briefly in blackface.

In other *Mickey Mouse* shorts, such racially charged humor appeared on the screen in a more sustained fashion. "Trader Mickey" (1932) is one of the *Mickey Mouse* episodes that ventures into serious, albeit well-worn, racial tropes. The short begins with Mickey and Pluto traveling on a steamboat filled with goods, and in a river filled with hippopotamuses. The hippos and the boat have the feel of scenes out of Joseph Conrad's *Heart of Darkness* (1899), as Mickey is clearly being situated in the other worldly context of Africa. Upon landing, Pluto discovers an odd black foot that turns out to belong to an indigenous African. This "savage" is represented in blackface and has bright white lips and a ring through his nose. Shortly thereafter, Mickey and Pluto find themselves surrounded by a large group of blackface spear-wielding natives, some with pulsating, evil-looking eyes. A rotund chief sits atop a pile of human skulls as he calls forth a cook to tend to a large cauldron. This scene establishes that these natives are also cannibals. Mickey attempts to speak to them, but the chief and cook respond in undecipherable gibberish. As they prepare to cook Mickey, the natives unsuccessfully attempt to use the goods on his ship. The chief, for instance, spies a cuckoo clock and attempts to eat the cuckoo. Others play musical instruments backward or use them improperly, all of which reinforces the cultural, as well as the biological and geographical space that is imagined to exist between Africa and American "civilization." Mickey, however, finally triumphs by securing a saxophone and playing it to subdue the "savages," who all join in singing and dancing.

The 1932 short "Trader Mickey" was rife with stereotypically racist images of black people. In their African setting, black people appear as "savages" with no history, or without language and the intelligence to record their own history. Depicted as apish blackface characters, they hatch a plan to eat Mickey, reinforcing the perception of Africans as cannibals. When they begin to play the musical instruments with Mickey, they all dance and gyrate in a "Negroid" fashion. As a "musical people," they are easily distracted by Mickey's music, ultimately forgetting that they had planned to eat him. Most importantly, as cultural historian Nicholas Sammond has observed, "Mickey's capture at the hands of these animated cannibals is an instance of cultural contact between a blackface minstrel (Mickey) and the less oblique racist stereotypes that historically had charged that figure with its libidinous, animalistic, and uncivilized appeal."[15]

Betty Boop also emerged in the early golden age period of cartoon production. Created by cartoon guru Max Fleischer, who also created *Popeye* and *Koko the Clown*, *Betty Boop* is most frequently critiqued for its sexism, not its racism.[16] The series contained racist elements that occasionally featured Betty as a racialized character. In "Betty Boop's Bamboo Isle" (1932), a brown-skinned Betty performed her version of a Polynesian hula dance. Her version of such a dance amounted to a parody of the hula, and her darkened skin implied a forged indigeneity.[17]

Like other cartoons of this period, *Betty Boop* frequently mocked nonwhite people, especially African Americans and Native Americans. As in *Mickey Mouse* or *Felix the Cat*, black people tend to appear in *Betty Boop* shorts as a backdrop or as comic relief. Take, for instance, the aforementioned "Betty Boop's Bamboo Isle." In that short, Betty's compatriot Bimbo lands on a proverbial desert island, where he encounters Betty. After a series of misadventures, a group of tribal islanders appear, their skins blackened, their teeth bright white, and bones tied in their hair. In addition, these island natives were depicted as having overly large and protruding lips. In an effort to impersonate the natives, Bimbo darkens his face with dirt and places a bone in his hair. He then chants an island-sounding song (which is actually performed by a real group, the Royal Samoans), in an effort to lead them away from Betty. As a result of his actions, Bimbo becomes the "chief" of this group. The islanders perform a series of odd dances, complete with whoops and grunts, to mark Bimbo's new position of authority. The natives, however, eventually discover they've been duped and chase Betty and Bimbo from the island.

"Making Stars" (1935) also contained blackface individuals, in this case a trio of pickaninnies called the Colorful Three. An Asian "star" added an additional element to the short's racism. In this episode, Betty introduces the stars of the future. The Colorful Three are exactly that: three pickaninnies with nappy hair adorned with bow ties, dark black skin, and overly large whitish/tannish lips. They crash and bang into one another until tears flow and they sing a lament in dialect called "hi de ho." The song is a riff on the classic Cab Calloway tune "Minnie the Moocher" (Calloway himself made several noteworthy appearances in *Betty Boop* shorts). To get the three pickaninnies off the stage a detached hand with a large plate of watermelon appears and successfully lures the Colorful Three away. As the crowd cheers its delight, the camera pans to the audience where a blackface "Mammy" and a pickaninny baby of her own sit clapping. The baby cries for his/her own "watermelon." Upon being "shooshed" by the "Mammy," the child begins singing its own version of "hi de ho." Finally tiring of this whining, the mother reaches into her purse and produces a large piece of watermelon, which the child devours. The next performer to appear is an Asian marksman. This Chinese-looking child has deeply "slanted" eyes and wears a queue. Stereotypical Asian-sounding music accompanies this act.

"Betty Boop's Bamboo Isle" and "Making Stars" offer rather standard stereotypical portrayals of blacks and Asians. The islanders in "Betty Boop's Bamboo Isle" were all blackface individuals with bones in their hair. They were unintelligent and easily tricked by Bimbo. They speak in grunts and were depicted solely as servants. The Colorful Three were similarly caricatured. They not only appeared as pickaninnies, but used a food item commonly associated with black people in Jim Crow America: watermelon. In this short, watermelon not only confounded the Colorful Three but also silenced the "Mammy's" crying child as all children devoured the watermelon with stereotypical gusto.[18]

Beyond blacks and Asians, the *Betty Boop* short "Rhythm on the Reservation" (1939) caricatured Native American people. This was the final short to feature *Betty Boop*, and it focused much of its attention on the Native American characters. In this episode, Betty drives down a road, her car filled with musical instruments, when she notices a sign for the "Wigwam Beauty Shoppe." On seeing the sign she remarks, "Oh, geez, real Indians." As she approaches the "Shoppe," she spots an advertisement, declaring: "Try Our Scalp Treatment." The female shopkeeper, a big-nosed, dark-skinned woman, notices Betty and attempts to rouse a male Native American who is sleeping. They both speak in "ugs" and grunts. The female Native American informs the big-nosed, dark-skinned male Native American that "ug, customer, makem ballyhoo!" Betty approaches the two and states: "Oh, how do you do, Mr. Redskin?" She proceeds to buy a tom-tom. Meanwhile, the rest of the "tribe," who also speak in "ugs" and grunts, prepare to rob Betty's car. The Native Americans attempt to use Betty's stolen instruments, much as in the *Mickey Mouse* short "Trader Mickey," but are unable to determine their use. She shows them how to make music.

"Rhythm on the Reservation" (1939) portrayed Native Americans as buffoonish, unintelligent, and prone to criminality. The short's hackneyed plot depicted indigenous people as lazy, backward "savages" who wanted nothing more than to pilfer Betty's car. But once the "Indians" have robbed Betty, the audience was reassured by the idea that they lacked the intelligence to properly play Betty's instruments. As in numerous other shorts from this period, "Rhythm on the Reservation" mocked and ridiculed indigenous people, feeding American audiences commonly held stereotypes about uncivilized natives in the form of entertainment.[19]

Many of the other popular series during the silent era and early golden age perpetuated similarly racist tropes. Although now largely forgotten, some of the other more popular cartoons of the 1920s and 1930s included several early shorts featuring Koko the Clown mimicking African Americans. Koko the Clown, a black and white character, replicated blackface caricatures that had been popular in the United States for many decades. In one notable episode, "St. James Infirmary Blues," (1933) Koko takes on an ethnic flare and sings with the legendary Cab Calloway. He dances and scats the song in a mockery of African American jazz and dance.

From the silent era to the opening years of the golden age of cartoons, demeaning portrayals of nonwhite people, especially people of African descent, were staples of the art form. But the period was also prototypical in the sense that animators from Max Fleischer to Otto Messmer to Walt Disney all set the stage for the types of popular accepted racist depictions of ethnic minorities that became commonplace during the golden age of animation. No other cartoon better represented the racist qualities of cartoon making in the United States than *Tom and Jerry*.

Tom and Jerry

Tom and Jerry first appeared in 1940. Like Mickey Mouse, the animated shorts became wildly popular with audiences. The shorts focused on the hijinks of Tom and Jerry, weaving into the plots immediately recognizable depictions of racial and ethnic minorities. Mammy Two Shoes became one of the most important of these figures. Her large, colorful dresses, thick southern accent, and dark-skinned appearance clearly indicated her racial alterity, and audiences saw her only from the waist or ankles down. Mammy Two Shoes was also portly, had large breasts, and thick legs and ankles. In many ways she represented the classic Mammy figure of popular culture.[20]

Mammy Two Shoes, voiced by Lillian Randolph, perhaps best known for playing "Annie" in *It's a Wonderful Life*, first appears in the 1940 inaugural *Tom and Jerry* cartoon "Puss Gets the Boot" (in which Tom and Jerry are referred to as "Jasper" and "Jinx"). As was routinely the case in *Tom and Jerry* cartoons, Tom terrorizes Jerry until Jerry finally escapes. When he attempts to once again catch Jerry, Tom instead crashes into a pedestal holding a potted plant, which in turn falls comically on his head. Mammy Two Shoes enters this chaotic scene wearing bright blue house shoes, red socks or panty hose, a yellow dress, with a white housekeeper's smock, and holding a broom. She tells him, "Now wood you jes look, jes look at dat mess you made … if you breaks one more thing you is going out. O W T, out." The subsequent scenes focus on Jerry attempting to break, or to cause Tom to break, household items so he will indeed be thrown "O W T, out" of the house. In the end, Tom breaks a large stack of dishes, forcing Mammy Two Shoes to evict him. She does so with her classic southern dialect, stating, "Mmmm, hmmm, and when I sez out, Jaspa, I means out. O W T, out."

"Puss Gets the Boot" typified how *Tom and Jerry* cartoons contained many of the trademark antics that came to define the series. What made this episode conform to prevailing racial stereotypes, however, was Mammy Two Shoes. Mammy Two Shoes was a racialized comedic foil, a brightly clad, broom-toting housekeeper who spoke in an uneducated dialect. Her image thus confirmed what most white people learned about the subordinate status of black women in American homes. While some episodes depicted Mammy Two Shoes in an even more grotesquely racist manner than her portrayal in "Puss Gets the Boot," this first episode set the tone for her appearances in future *Tom and Jerry* cartoons.

Mammy Two Shoes returned in the second *Tom and Jerry* short, "The Midnight Snack" (1941). In this episode, the cat and mouse fight over a fridge full of delectable food until a wedge of cheese crashes into some dishes, breaking them in the process. Mammy Two Shoes enters the scene of commotion and warns Tom, "Cat, if yous been in dat ice box, start prayin!" Tom then places Jerry in the refrigerator, framing the mouse for eating the food. Upon discovering Jerry, Mammy Two Shoes, brightly clad with blue house shoes, red and white striped stockings, and a yellow dress with white smock, screams, jumps up on a chair, and proceeds to raise her yellow dress along with approximately 10 other dresses—one with bright yellow and blue stripes, another with light blue stars, one with green polka dots, and finally a black and white checkered dress—before calling Tom to the rescue. In the process of trying to get Jerry, Tom accidentally knocks Mammy Two Shoes off of her chair. She runs off, exclaiming, "This here's no place fo a lady!" When Tom fails to catch Jerry, Mammy Two Shoes decides to evict Tom from the home.

Many of the stock images introduced in "Puss Gets the Boot" reappeared in "The Midnight Snack." Mammy Two Shoes was once again a large, dark black, colorfully dressed woman. Added to this short are her numerous dresses, all worn inexplicably at the same time, and all garish in their colors and patterns. Thus, her attire constituted a form of humorous mockery. A gendered element of mockery was added when Mammy Two Shoes fled the kitchen, exclaiming, "This here's no place fo a lady!" According to the stereotypes of the time, black women were not afforded the title, much less the social privileges, of "lady." Such scenes therefore served as a form of comedic relief in which all the white viewers were in on the joke.

Mammy Two Shoes made perhaps her most important appearance in the 1950 short "Saturday Evening Puss." This cartoon began with Tom spying on Mammy Two Shoes as she readied herself for a night out at a bridge game. Her choice of clothes and jewelry were, as in previous versions, a source of ridicule and humor. In this instance, she wore a vibrant blue dress with bright green trim around the waist and sleeves. She donned 10 or so brightly colored bracelets, four rings, and a very large necklace with a red and green broach. The action pauses momentarily on the broach, which chimes, while the top red portion of the broach lights up with word "stop" and the bottom green portion chimes with the word "go." Here the message is simple: the broach is so garishly large that it could serve as a traffic signal. After hiking up her slip in an unladylike fashion, Mammy Two Shoes "galumphed" when she walks out the door, leaving Tom alone. Seeing his chance, Tom invites three friends for a party, and they proceed to play loud jazz music. Jerry, tortured by this music and desiring only sleep, battles the cats until he finally calls Mammy Two Shoes at her bridge game to inform her of the party. She hurries home to expel Tom and his friends.

What makes "Saturday Evening Puss" especially important is that for the first and only time in the series, Mammy Two Shoes was shown from head to toe. As she races from the bridge game, down the street, and home, in a split second her full body is visible. Her rotundness clearly evident, her large bosoms, oversized nose, swollen cheeks, bright red lipstick, and a bright red hat all serve as indicators of her lack of physical symmetry and, thus, racial inferiority. Moreover, her hands, shown at the beginning of the episode as she dressed and later when she expels the cats, appear dark black on top but a light brown on her palms, much like the paws of an animal. Thus, her hands reminded viewers of her more animalistic nature, something that was in stark contrast to how white Americans saw themselves.

In communicating racist stereotypes about black people, and African American women specifically, the Mammy Two Shoes character had much to say. Her exaggerated, "Negroid" features caricatured the black body in much the same way that nineteenth-century depictions of dark black, white-teeth grinning Mammies and Sambos served to ridicule black people on the minstrel stage. Her southern accent and dialect clearly communicated both a class and racial position of inferiority, while her bright, colorful clothing and jewelry all fit into prevailing stereotypes about black women's love of tacky, brightly colored clothes. The racialized imagery used in representing Mammy Two Shoes had become so ubiquitous in American popular culture by the 1940s and 1950s that whites often overlooked the offensive nature of such representations. Author Thomas Pluck gave voice to this aspect of white privilege when he remembered Mammy Two Shoes fondly, stating: "I never felt there was a cruelty in how 'Mammy Two Shoes' was portrayed." Pluck continued, noting that many groups were caricatured by the media and he lists the Irish cop or Italian gangsters as commonly stereotyped figures. Pluck's analysis simplistically creates a sense of cultural equivalence in the derogatory ways in which people of African and/or Irish descent were portrayed in cartoons during the mid-twentieth century. The racial context in which Mammy Two Shoes was portrayed made it particularly difficult for upward social and economic mobility in African American communities. In contrast, Irish immigrants, and their children and grandchildren, could bank on their "wages of whiteness" assisting them in rising up the U.S. social and economic ladder, a point Pluck appears to miss. In other words, Mammy Two Shoes reinforced perceptions of African

American people, and black women in particular, as stuck in a subordinate, servile status in American society.[21]

The racism embedded in mid-twentieth century America ran through *Tom and Jerry* episodes. One short, which was ultimately deemed so offensive that it was banned from TV, was the 1951 cartoon "His Mouse Friday." In this episode, Tom, adrift on a raft in the ocean, lands on a "deserted" island. Thinking he is alone, Tom soon discovers that Jerry is also on the island. Tom chases Jerry into an indigenous village. Jerry then darkens his face with soot from a large pot. He jumps from the forest, now totally blackened, wearing a yellow loin cloth, holding a spear, with a bone tied in his hair, and speaking a strange gibberish to Tom. He forces Tom to the large pot where he will seemingly cook the cat as his dinner. Tom discovers Jerry's trick and chases him from the village, only to run into the actual village inhabitants, who are very black "natives" (with the Mammy Two Shoes–like brightly colored jewelry, clothes, and hair), catlike in appearance—hence cannibals—one of whom exclaims "barbecued cat" while licking his lips. Tom runs while the natives, most of whom are seen only by their feet, give chase. Jerry smiles at Tom's fate, only to encounter a large, "Negroid"-like mouse, who says "barbecued mouse" while licking his lips. Jerry then flees this "cannibal."

In the case of "His Mouse Friday," *Tom and Jerry* ventured into a slightly more all-inclusive form of racism. Jerry is in blackface and uses his disguise to trick Tom. Reinforcing the image of the islanders' racial inferiority, dark-skinned natives and their bright jewels and clothing remind viewers of Mammy Two Shoes. Visually, the cartoon focuses on the islanders' feet, in much the same way the animators focused on Mammy Two Shoes feet to demarcate a subservient status, with the added joke that plays on popular perceptions of Pacific Islanders as cannibals. "His Mouse Friday" was therefore an amalgam of blackface minstrelsy and caricatures about island cannibalism, racial stereotypes that white privilege in mid-twentieth-century America rendered humorous.

There are a number of other ways in which black people were ridiculed and mocked in *Tom and Jerry* cartoons. In many episodes, an explosion or some accident with mud or paint leaves Tom, Jerry, or other characters blackened, and they turn to the audience in blackface for a brief moment before returning to their normal coloration. Take "Yankee Doodle Mouse" (1943), for example. This short, which won the Academy Award for Best Animated Short Film, finds Tom and Jerry in a World War II–type battle. In one scene, Tom attempts to "bomb" Jerry with firecrackers. One firecracker lands in a tea kettle where Jerry is hiding. Tom looks inside as the firework explodes, leaving his face blackened and the remains of the teapot haloed around his head. He looks at the audience momentarily before resuming his hunt for Jerry. In another well-known episode, "Mouse in Manhattan" (1945), Jerry visits New York City and falls into an open container of shoe polish, leaving his face blackened and for unknown reasons his lips larger and bright red. In a more easily noticeable episode, "The Truce Hurts" (1947), Tom, Jerry, and their canine compatriot Spike make a truce to be friends. In one scene, a passing meat truck drenches the three in mud. Once the truck passes, Spike, Tom, and Jerry look out at the audience with their faces blackened and bows in their hair, a depiction akin to that of a pickaninny. Again, the reference to blackface minstrelsy in all of these episodes is obvious. Upon close scrutiny, these blackface portrayals in *Tom and Jerry* are so common and obvious that they can begin to seem normative. We would argue that that is because they were normative, common representations of black people, marketed mainly to white audiences.[22]

But *Tom and Jerry* did not solely mock African Americans. Indeed, the cartoon frequently lampooned Native Americans and Latinos and, on occasion, Asian Americans also. Perhaps the most extreme form of racism toward Native Americans came in the 1952 short "Two Little Indians." In this episode, two gray mice (both resembling the recurring character Nibbles, albeit wearing headbands with feathers and each sporting a small bow and arrow) approach Jerry's home, knock on his door, and hand him a note that states they are orphans from the "Bide-a-wee Mouse Home" (interestingly, Bideawee is the name of an actual animal shelter founded in 1906 in New York City, although the "Two Little Indians" writers most likely chose the name because it sounded "Indian" and evoked the many isolated boarding schools established for indigenous children by the federal government).[23] Jerry takes the two on a hike, during which they encounter Tom. One of the two attempts to "scalp" Tom with a large axe. The other attacks Tom while performing the hand-on-mouth Indian whoop cry. Tom is eventually scalped, but succeeds in capturing Jerry. The two little Native Americans then trick Tom into thinking he is surrounded by natives; he dons a coonskin cap and grabs a black powder rifle to defend himself. To scare Tom, the two little Native Americans also doll up Spike the dog to look like a Native American chief. Finally outwitted, Tom raises a white flag and the short ends with Tom, Jerry, and the two little Native Americans smoking a peace pipe. The episode's bigotry and use of racial generalizations is completed via the Native American–sounding music and the beating of tom-tom drums that are heard throughout the short.

Like many of the blackface episodes of *Tom and Jerry*, "Two Little Indians" incorporates virtually every Native American stereotype in American popular culture. It is a classic example of redface entertainment. The two attempts at scalping Tom—one successful, one not—are good examples, as are the peace pipe, the music and drums, and the war whoop cry. When Tom dresses in the coonskin cap and grabs a gun, the cowboys and Native Americans motif is complete, if historically inaccurate.[24] As in numerous cowboy and Native American movies, the battle in "Two Little Indians" featured savage braves, mice that seemingly want to harm Tom only because he is a cat, and the cowboy figure of Tom. As in many episodes of *Tom and Jerry*, Tom loses, an important difference between many cowboy and Native American films in which the Native Americans usually lose.

Native Americans make only a handful of appearances in other episodes of *Tom and Jerry*. In many of these shorts, their appearance is akin to the brief appearances of Tom or Jerry in blackface after an explosion. In the 1945 episode "The Mouse Comes to Dinner" (which also features Mammy Two Shoes dressed as a maid), Jerry attempts to steal food from a dinner table. He grabs some onion tops to hide behind and runs inside a napkin, which is folded to look like a teepee. When Jerry pokes his head out of the napkin to see if the coast is clear, the onion tops are now on his head in an approximation of a Native American feather headdress. In another instance of redface, it is Tom who appears like a Native American. "Flirty Bird" from 1945 features Tom matching wits with a large red bird. In one scene, this bird throws Tom, who flies through a sheet on a clothesline and onto a bucket next to a feather duster. The feather duster, clothespins from the clothesline, and sheet are rearranged on Tom, who now looks like a cigar-store Indian with a feather headdress, Indian blanket, with the clothespins held like cigars. Like many of the blackface episodes, the ridiculing of Native Americans follows a standard pattern that was by the 1940s centuries old.

Latinos appear with less frequency in *Tom and Jerry* cartoons, but one that does make reference to Latinos is the 1957 short "Mucho Mouse." While this episode is ostensibly located in Spain, the racial stereotypes and accents sound Mexican. The episode begins with an orange cat strumming a guitar as Jerry, a.k.a. "El Magnífico," openly steals cheese. The lady of the house, known as "Joan," demands that the cat chase the mouse. He is consistently foiled by El Magnífico. The orange cat explains, "It is no use," to which Joan responds, "It is no use? Porque usted lazy [because you are lazy]. Of all the lazy cats I have ever seen, you are the most lazy, lazy, lazy!" "Yo lazy!" The cat responds, "Señorita you have hurt me here [he points to his heart] … nadie, absolutely no one can catch El Magnífico." Joan, therefore, calls in reinforcements: Tom. Upon his arrival, Tom battles El Magnífico for some time—at one point Jerry becomes a bull fighter and Tom a bull—until Tom finally capitulates. Joan returns home to find Tom and the orange cat both strumming on guitars. She asks, "Qué pasa aquí what's going on here," to which the orange cat responds, "Señorita, I told you, no one, but no one can catch El Magnífico." He looks toward Tom and asks, "No es verdad amigo [isn't that right friend]?" Tom replies, "Sí, es verdad amigo," and the two go on playing their guitars while Jerry steals several pieces of fruit.

A similar caricaturing of Latinos appears in other *Tom and Jerry* episodes. In "Baby Puss" (1943), a little girl, "Nancy," forces Tom to act like a baby. Several of Tom's alley cat friends, Butch/Dreamboy, Topsy, and Meathead, witness his baby-like behavior and begin to make fun of Tom. They do so by dancing and playing makeshift musical instruments, while Topsy dons a red skirt, bright red lipstick, purplish eye shadow, and a large fruit hat and does a rendition of Carmen Miranda singing "Mamãe eu quero" (mama I want). The song itself is sung in a silly, mocking manner, but it is Topsy's appropriation of Miranda that strikes a racist chord. This Latino-face depiction appropriates the most stereotypical aspects of a prominent Latina.

The bigotry in "Mucho Mouse" and "Baby Puss" may have escaped critical viewers since one episode was centered in Spain and the other was a rather brief appearance of Latinoface, but all of the stereotypes evident in the cartoon were clearly those applied for generations to Mexican-origin people and other Latinos. The two most important stereotypes in "Mucho Mouse" were the broken, Spanglish dialog of the orange cat and Joan and the repeated references/allusions to laziness. As numerous Latino scholars have shown, one of the most incomprehensible stereotypes directed at Latinos in general, and Mexican Americans specifically, was laziness.[25] Here the orange cat has clearly given up trying to catch El Magnífico, so Joan calls him lazy not once but several times. So pervasive is this laziness that Tom is ultimately corrupted by it after failing to catch Jerry/El Magnífico. The additional elements of the bull fight and the Latin music that plays throughout (usually the famous piece España Cañi by Pascual Marquina Narro) all add to the stereotypical feel of the episode. In "Baby Puss" we have the appearance of brownface minstrelsy. Much like the other blackface depictions in *Tom and Jerry*, Topsy adopts the most over-the-top, exaggerated features of Carmen Miranda (and other famous Latinas) in order to make their appearance comical.

Stereotypical depictions of Asian Americans appear even less frequently than those of Latinos in *Tom and Jerry*. Yellowface representations almost always showcased the conical Asian hat, a Fu Manchu mustache, and occasionally "slanted" epicanthic fold eyes. In one of the original episodes, "Puss n' Toots" (1942), Tom and Jerry fight on a large automatic record player. Jerry is able to trap Tom on the turntable and then change records. A large swing arm brings a record crashing upon Tom's head, at which point a gong sounds. The scene cuts to Tom, now spinning on the turntable, Buddha-like, with the record as his Asian hat, a Fu Manchu mustache, and "slanted" eyes. The scene is completed with "Oriental"-sounding music and Jerry dancing about before bowing to the audience. In comparison, "Little Runaway" (1952) features an escaped seal who tosses Tom into a bird feeder, which crashes down upon him. The bowl of the bird feeder lands on Tom's head, once again with a gong, as Asian-sounding music plays. Tom is left with the bowl on his head, which approximate the Asian conical hat, his yellowface appearance completed by a Fu Manchu mustache and epicanthic fold eyes.

No other cartoon of the golden age quite matched the level of importance, popularity, and longevity as *Tom and Jerry*. The series both replicated the most common racist stereotypes of previous media forms, while also educating generations of children on the racial etiquette of mid-twentieth-century racism. However, while racist depictions featured heavily in the series, nothing in *Tom and Jerry* came close to touching the racism that was so evident in the banned cartoons of the era.

The Censored Eleven and Other Banned Cartoons

At about the same time that *Tom and Jerry* became popular, *Merrie Melodies* and *Looney Tunes*, both originally produced by Warner Brothers and later by Associated Artists Productions (AAP), released cartoons that contained explicitly racist content.[26] Many of these shorts were later banned by United Artists (the parent company that acquired *Merrie Melodies* and *Looney Tunes*); they have come to be known as the Censored Eleven.[27]

One of the earliest of the Censored Eleven was "Hittin' the Trail for Hallelujah Land" (1931). This short featured a Mickey Mouse knockoff named "Piggy," who, like the original "Steamboat Willie," piloted a paddlewheel steamboat. The short begins with a group of blackface individuals singing about "Hittin' the Trail for Hallelujah Land." This is a clear riff on popular black jazz at the time. The short then cuts to a wagon driven by an older African American gentleman. His passenger is Fluffy, Piggy's girlfriend. At one point, the paddlewheel's whistle blows, and Fluffy states, "Oh there's the boat, hurry Uncle Tom." Uncle Tom's white beard, large lips, and speech that is almost indecipherable represent a racialized character so often seen in other blackface depictions. To reinforce Uncle Tom's subordinate status, he is portrayed as subservient to Fluffy, obeying her with a kindness and grace befitting his name. The short proceeds with Uncle Tom successfully delivering Fluffy to Piggy's boat. But then Uncle Tom runs into trouble when he encounters a group of clearly "Negro" skeletons at a cemetery. They too sing that they will help Uncle Tom get to "Hallelujah Land." He escapes and ends up nearly drowning in a river, his life saved by Piggy.[28]

As in several of the cartoons discussed earlier, the stereotypical depictions of African Americans in "Hittin' the Trail for Hallelujah Land" followed a familiar racialized format. The jazz band and its music, as well as Uncle Tom and the skeletons, all represent black people as easy going, foolhardy, big lipped, and slow speaking. Tom's reaction to the skeletons implies the superstitious nature of black people. He also cannot swim. The racism is thus explicit.

Friz Freleng directed two of the better-known Censored Eleven cartoons. Freleng actually developed several of the most famous prejudicial cartoon characters, especially Speedy Gonzales, discussed later. In 1936 he directed the second of the Censored Eleven, a racist cartoon titled "Sunday Go to Meetin' Time." In this short, church bells sound as a very large, white-lipped, dark-skinned minister welcomes congregants to church with what sounds like an old-style spiritual. Several black people venture into the church, including a large woman who resembles a Mammy-type character. The scene's racialized context is enhanced by an elderly black man with large lips and bulging eyes as he sits in a rocking chair ringing the church bells. The focus of the scene then shifts to a black couple on their way to the church. They modify the preacher's song with a more upbeat, jazzy tune. They are also dressed in stereotypical fashion, she in a bright green dress and he in a zoot suit; both have the same dark skin, bulging lips, and bright eyes; and they saunter in a kind of walking dance.

"Sunday Go to Meetin' Time" also represented other members of the community readying themselves for church. In one scene, a larger, Mammy-like black woman inspects her pickaninny children. She applies shoe polish to their bald heads so that a man, presumably her husband, can polish them to a shine as though performing a shoeshine. All of these figures once again have dark skin, overly large white lips, and exaggerated facial features. Another large black woman with even larger lips and wearing a green dress and a hat with a large feather emerges from her home calling to a "Nicodemus." She finds him shooting dice and commands that he accompany her to church, calls him "lazy" and "shiftless," and drags him by the ear when he does not want to go. "Dat church be dere next week," he says, while Gospel-sounding music plays. He is able to sneak out of church, but is knocked unconscious chasing a chicken. He ends up in the Hades Court of Justice, where a Sambo-looking judge finds Nicodemus guilty of sin and sends him to hell. A group of big-lipped demons then escort him to the devil. "Oh you got to give the devil his due," the devil sings, and the demons begin poking Nicodemus with pitchforks as his punishment. He awakes and rushes to church having learned his lesson.

"Sunday Go to Meetin' Time" represented African American Christianity in bufoonish terms, Nicodemus serving to highlight the questionable nature of black religiosity as white Americans perceived it. Almost every single character in the short appears as a blackface pickaninny, Sambo, or Mammy. As in other shorts, they all wear brightly colored, somewhat outlandish clothing that clearly appears to be beyond the class position of the individuals in the cartoon and indicates to viewers how black people try too hard to ape the styles of wealthy white people. In this short, the characters all have dark skin with light brown palms, which makes their hands appear more paw or animal-like than human. The protagonist is named "Nicodemus," perhaps a name as stereotypical in its origins as "Uncle Tom" or "Sambo." He, like "Tex's Coon" (discussed later), is a slow-witted, lower-class "Negro" who would rather toss dice than go to church.

Friz Freleng directed four of the Censored Eleven, giving him the record of having directed the most of these banned films. His other works followed many of the same racist patterns established in "Sunday Go to Meetin' Time." For example, "Clean Pastures" (1937) mocks Depression-era Harlem. In a similarly mocking tone, "Jungle Jitters" (1938) depicts the fate of a traveling salesman who encounters a group of "African" tribespeople. And lastly, Freleng directed the 1944 short "Goldilocks and the Jivin' Bears," which featured a group of musical, blackface bears who cannot stop playing their instruments and are always on the lookout for a party. This short combined the nursery rhymes associated with the Goldilocks story, Little Red Riding Hood, and Freleng's racist depiction of African American jazz culture. Of Freleng's banned shorts, "Clean Pastures" merits further attention.

"Clean Pastures" mimics 1930s' Harlem, a moment when the city "was en vogue" and jazz music and speakeasies brought the city to life at night. For Freleng, this festive atmosphere was something to be parodied. The film opens with a group of scantily clad black women dancing in a chorus line. They all have big lips coated with dark red lipstick. The jazz playing in the background moves to a fast tempo, although in later scenes it will transition to Gospel music. There are also shots of black hands rolling dice and shaking a martini; all of these hands are dark but for their palms, which are light, again approximating the paws of animals and not the hands of human beings. The opening scenes also depict a couple dancing; both speak outlandishly; their dancing is exaggerated and "exotic"; and they both have big lips and broad and toothy grins and wear brightly colored clothes—she in a red dress, he in a purplish zoot suit with a pink hat. These opening scenes set the stage for the latter parts of the short, which like "Sunday Go to Meetin' Time" focuses on a kind of parodied Christian morality.

The film pans into outer space and gives the audience a glimpse of heaven, which also gets lampooned. Above the pearly gates a sign reads "Pair-o-Dice." An older, large, Uncle Tom–like black angel, with Freleng's now well-established Negro accoutrements—dark skin, overly large lips, and lightly brown paw-like palms—reads a newspaper that indicates that the stock of heaven has been losing ground to "Hades, Inc." This Uncle Tom or black Saint Peter telephones another taller angel, who seems to be practicing playing the trumpet. This individual also has very large lips and a sloping forehead, and he seems incapable of closing his mouth, giving him a lethargic appearance that is clearly designed to show that he is unintelligent. He is the cartoon version of Stepin Fetchit, the pseudonym of African American actor Lincoln Perry, who, as we noted in Chapter 3, often played roles as a slow-witted, lazy, barely intelligible black man. This cartoon Stepin Fetchit finally answers the phone with a slow, southern drawl; "Yaaaasssuuuuh, Haaarwuhm? Uh right now? Yaaaasssuuuuh, okey dokey bawss." He then returns to practicing the trumpet as the phone rings again, this time more insistently. The tall angel jumps to his feet and begins running, only to slow down after just a few moments.

This tall, Stepin Fetchit angel, who never seems capable of closing his mouth, evidently plans to save the fate of Pair-o-Dice by becoming a street-corner preacher. A host of stereotypical blackface individuals walk by, ignoring the angel as he buffoonishly tries to implore them to listen. He is unable to read his own sign, which instructs people to help Pair-o-Dice (and advertises that one of heaven's benefits is watermelon). Several of the passersby are obvious parodies of real-life performers. One individual tap dances by the angel, a clear mockery of Bill Robinson's "Bojangles" character. Another, shorter blackface individual riffs on Al Jolson's blackface from *The Jazz Singer*. The tall angel is incapable of preventing the Jolson character, and presumably all the others, from entering bars or dance houses. Back in heaven, a group of four other angels, all blackface approximations of other prominent black entertainers—Cab Calloway, Jim Lunceford, Louis Armstrong, Fats Waller—appeal to the blackface Saint Peter to allow them to help save Harlem. He consents, and the four put on a jazz show that wows audiences. Harlem, en masse, follows this jazz group to Pair-o-Dice. Saint Peter hangs a "no vacancies" sign, but there is a knock at the door. It's none other than a blackface devil, who asks to come in. Evidently Hade's Inc. had been put out of business by Pair-o-Dice.

As in Freleng's other racist shorts, "Clean Pastures" reduces all black people to big-lipped, party-loving, slow-witted Sambos, Uncle Toms, and Mammies. The Stepin Fetchit–like tall angel is the most clearly offensive, confirming for the audiences the supposed intellectual, moral, and physical inferiority of all African Americans. But this cartoon also does something different: it lampoons real-life individuals. Most other cartoons of this era that ridiculed black people did not take as their subjects actual African Americans. "Clean Pastures" differs in that it specifically references prominent stars such as Cab Calloway or Bill Robinson, in many ways confirming not only the potential threat of black Americans and their forms of entertainment but also the real-life threat posed by actual black people.

Warner Brothers and *Merrie Melodies* continued its cartoon racism with the 1941 short "All This and Rabbit Stew," featuring Bugs Bunny and a slow-witted pickaninny. The unnamed African American child, a black approximation of Elmer Fudd, has dark black skin but overly large tan-colored lips. He has an oblong head complete with a very large forehead. He wears overalls with a red bandana tied around his neck and oversized, almost clown-like shoes that he always seems on the verge of tripping over. He is oafish and clumsy, drags his gun by the barrel, walks very slowly, and speaks with a drawl. He is, in short, a young pickaninny Sambo. When the short begins, for instance, he is singing a song lazily, "I'se gonna ca-ha-ha-hach me a ra-ha-ha-habit, mmm, hmmm, ma-hahah-hmm, gonna ca-ha-ha-hach me a ra-ha-ha-habit, mmm, hmmm, ma-hahah-hmm." When he comes across Bugs's hole he stops and says, "Well, shut my mouf, rabbit twacks." Throughout most of the episode he chases Bugs with the hope of securing his dinner. When he finally seems to have cornered Bugs, the rabbit produces a pair of dice, which mesmerize the hunter. He cannot resist a game of dice. Hidden behind a bush, they play several games; Bugs wins, and he emerges from the bush wearing the hunter's clothes and dragging his gun. The hunter is left naked, covered only by a grape leaf, and he remarks to the audience, "Wayell, call me Adam." As the cartoon closes Bugs even takes the grape leaf.

The hunter is identified as "Tex's Coon" only after the short ends. The reference here is to Tex Avery, who produced many of the racist pieces of animation discussed earlier. Like other cartoons during this period, this episode appealed to popularly held racial prejudices. First, notice the possession of Avery over the character; it is Tex's Coon, not a real character in his own right. Of course, "coon" is also a racist epithet for black people. The lazy, slow-witted aspects of the hunter ridicule black people as stereotypically indolent and unintelligent, evidenced by the way the hunter cannot come close to cornering Bugs. His slang and drawl also convey his level of intelligence. He is also prone to criminality and cannot prevent himself from gambling, the game of dice used as a cultural shorthand to reference the excessive amounts of gambling that whites perceived African Americans partaking in during the Jim Crow era.

The most notorious of the Censored Eleven shorts was "Coal Black and de Sebben Dwarfs" (1943), which parodied Disney's very popular *Snow White* feature film. The short begins with a large black woman rocking a child before bedtime. She asks the child, in a clearly outlandish black female voice, "Oh honey child, what story would you like to have Mammy tell you tonight?" The child asks to hear about So White and de Sebben Dwarfs. The short then cuts to the Evil or Wicked Queen's castle. The Evil Queen, it turns out, is a dark black, big-lipped, big-breasted woman, who asks the magic mirror to send her a prince. Garish-sounding jazz music plays while a car drives up to the castle carrying "Prince Chawmin." He is another large-lipped individual, who speaks in rhymes and wears a bright white zoot suit. The short cuts again to a younger black woman, who wears a very short skirt and is bent over a washtub with her backside pointed at the audience. She turns and says, "My hair is coal black but my name is So White." She also asks for a prince, and so Prince Chawmin arrives and they begin to dance. Enraged, the Evil Queen calls Murder Inc. to kill So White—their motto is that they'll kill anyone for $1, midgets for half price, and "Japs" for free. Fortunately, the Murder Inc. crew, another group of blackface individuals, release So White. They have lipstick kiss marks on their rather large lips, hinting that So White performed some type of sexual act to earn her release.

So White ventures into a dark forest, where she is befriended by "de Seb-ben Dwarfs," a group of military-like soldiers (who are all blackface little people). They make her their camp cook. Meanwhile, the Queen plans to poison So White with an apple, one that even contains a blackface apple worm and his family. When the barely disguised Queen gives the apple to So White, she eats it whole and faints. Prince Chawmin attempts to revive her with a kiss but fails. Instead, it is the smallest dwarf who kisses and saves her. Prince Chawmin asks him, "Man, what you got that makes So White think you so hot?" The diminutive dwarf responds, "Well dat is a military secret." The short closes with the Mammy figure still rocking the child.[29]

The racism in "Coal Black and de Sebben Dwarfs" is unparalleled in cartoon history. This short throws virtually every black stereotype into the mix, beginning with the Mammy character, who, while in shadow, is clearly a large black woman with a distinct "Negroid" voice. The child is a big-cheeked pickaninny with a bow in her hair. The Queen is a very large black woman, but asexual, with a deep, masculine voice, small eyes, and large lips accentuated by bright red lipstick that cannot cover all of her lips. She is dressed in lime green dress with red-and-white-striped hose. The Prince is a similarly caricatured black man: he has straightened hair, wears a white zoot suit and a monocle, and has gold teeth (his two front teeth are dominoes). So White is portrayed as a hypersexual, big-bottomed younger black woman, with perky bosoms and revealing clothing. She is less representative of blackface characters and instead represents the black Jezebel or whore, voluptuous, lascivious, and sexually available. She is the object of every character's sexual desire, except the Queen, and her sex appeal reminds the audience of the purported exoticness of some black women. Her escape from Murder Inc., also represented by four blackface darky characters, is predicated on So White having performed sexual acts to gain her freedom. The Sebben Dwarfs are also blackface representations. As in the Snow White story, the titular character can be revived only by a kiss—in Disney's version "true love's kiss." In this version, the kiss is a much more passionate and sexual embrace. Chawmin fails at this, but the smallest dwarf succeeds, his kiss being so powerful it lifts So White off the ground and she immediately falls in love with him. Thus, the ultimate seductive power—and what inspired the racial anxieties of millions of white men—of the black man, and black woman, is confirmed in this brief cartoon.

The other Censored Eleven cartoons all follow the patterns established in the episodes mentioned earlier. Of the other 11, Avery's "Uncle Tom's Bungalow" (1937) and Freleng's "Goldilocks and the Jivin' Bears" (1944) most closely resemble the blackface darky humor of the likes of "Clean Pastures" and "Coal Black and de Sebben Dwarfs." Other shorts, such as the 1944 short "Angel Puss," directed by Chuck Jones, later of *Tom and Jerry* fame, offer up a big-lipped black pickaninny named "Sambo." The Censored Eleven were banned and removed from circulation in the 1960s because they were deemed by censors to be far too racist for popular consumption. While the directors of these cartoons went on to portray different forms of racism in cartoons, the banning of these shorts indicated that cultural attitudes about race and racism had shifted considerably.

Reflective of these changing times, a number of animation studios and their distributors effectively banned offensive cartoons. These shorts were never officially restricted; rather, they were unofficially banned by television networks who refused to show them. Like "All This and Rabbit Stew," numerous other *Looney Tunes* shorts featured stereotypical depictions of a variety of ethnic groups. *Looney Tunes* directors such as Bob Clampett, Friz Freleng, and Tex Avery directed many of the racist Censored Eleven, so it is perhaps unsurprising that audiences might encounter ethnic bigotry in other *Looney Tunes* shorts. Take, for instance, "Tokio Jokio" (1943) and "Bugs Bunny Nips the Nips" (1944) both of which contain numerous World War II–era anti-Japanese messages.[30] "Tokio Jokio" opens with stereotypical-sounding Japanese music and a rooster about to crow. The rooster removes its skin and is instead a buzzard with Japanese yellowface features: big teeth, "slanted" eyes, and says, "uh, carkle doordle doo, preeze." The film constituted a classic piece of anti-Japanese propaganda. It features a series of vignettes mocking the Japanese; their advanced air raid siren, which is really one yellowface man poking another yellowface man in the backside with a pin; a Japanese "aircraft spotter" who is big toothed and "slanty" eyed and wearing glasses; and in "Kitchen Hints" a short, big-lipped, yellowface "Prof. Tojo," explaining how to make a Japanese club sandwich by stacking bread and meat ration cards. Throughout the short, Japanese individuals appear in yellowface and when they speak they always substitute an "R" for an "L." For example, a sportscaster named Red Toga-San offers "high-rights in the world of sports." In the next scene we see Yamamoto in "head-rine personalities." All of the characters are depicted as buffoonish, incompetent, and primitive.

In "Bugs Bunny Nips the Nips," Bugs floats in a box in the Pacific Ocean. He happens upon what appears to be a deserted island, but soon the island is under attack. Bugs hides in a haystack that a Japanese soldier already occupies. He has typical yellowface features: he is short, has buck teeth and epicanthic fold eyes, and wears glasses. He speaks in a Japanese-sounding gibberish. Bugs also encounters a Japanese sumo wrestler, whom he wrestles and ultimately defeats by dressing as a geisha. Bugs then sees an invasion force and remarks: "Japs, hundreds of em." He attempts to stop these soldiers by handing them ice cream–covered grenades. The soldiers, again all yellowface caricatures of the Japanese, rush in for their ice cream. Bugs readily passes out these treats, calling many of the soldiers by ethnic slurs, "here you are, here's yours bow legs. Here, one for you, monkey face. Don't shove.… Here you are, slant eyes." The bombs explode, defeating the enemy.

The production of anti-Japanese cartoons and films was generally consistent with American wartime propaganda throughout this period. The Japanese were frequently portrayed negatively as a primitive, incompetent, and substandard enemy. The depictions were usually built on popular yellowface portrayals that mocked the appearance of the Japanese. In both "Tokio Jokio" and "Bugs Bunny Nips the Nips," however, we have added elements, such as the mocking of language, either through Japanese-sounding gibberish or through the poor English language skills of the soldiers, as well as the demeaning name calling done by Bugs Bunny himself. In the end, even a rascally rabbit can defeat the Japanese.

Many of the *Looney Tunes/Merrie Melodies* directors independently produced their own racist characters and cartoon shorts. These include Clampett's "Porky Pig" and Freleng's "Speedy Gonzales." For example, in "Scalp Trouble" (1939) the object of Clampett's ire is Native Americans. Daffy Duck and Porky Pig are soldiers at a western fort. A group of stereotypical redface Native Americans are called by a large siren (that has a hand so that it can provide the hand-to-mouth war whoop Indian cry) to battle. "Injuns, the Indians are a, a, a … mohican, Redskins!" Porky shouts, trying to get the attention of other soldiers. One soldier picks off Native Americans on horseback with ease. To gain an upper hand, one Native soldier pulls out a bottle of "Four Noses Fire Water," drinks it, and then uses what appears to be his own fiery breath to burn a hole in the walls of the fort. Another soldier at the fort fires his gun while singing "Ten Little Indians" as he marks off his kills on a chalkboard. Similar stereotypes pervade "Pilgrim Porky" (1940), which features the pig on the Mayflower. He lands to find a redface version of Sitting Bull waiting for his arrival. Similarly, in "Injun Trouble" (1938), later remade in color as "Wagon Heels" (1945), Porky leads a wagon train into "Injun Joe's Territory." The character "Injun Joe" is a brawny, fierce warrior with a large red nose and eyes covered by his braided hair. He is a riff on the classic "fierce warrior" Indian motif. He finally catches Porky and is about to scalp him when another character, "Sloppy Moe," who has happened by at several moments during the short, appears again singing "I know something I won't tell" to the tune of "London Bridge is Falling Down." The Native American grabs Sloppy Moe and asks, "What you know, huh?" Moe replies, "Injun Joe is ticklish," and he tickles Injun Joe, who falls off a cliff. When he hits the ground, the earth is sucked down into the hole he creates, changing the map of the land. Before, the United States was just a sliver on the map, but with the vortex created by Injun Joe's fall, the United States is pulled across the continent.

Like Clampett, Freleng produced his own anti-Indian cartoons. In "Tom Tom Tomcat," for example, released in 1939, Tweety and Granny ride in a wagon across a desert. A Native American, really Sylvester the Cat with a feathered headband, notices the wagon and sends up smoke signals. The signals are seen by a group of Sylvester-looking Native Americans, who whoop and holler while Indian drums are played. They attack, and Granny shouts, "Heavens to Betsy, Injuns!" She and Tweety escape into an abandoned fort, and Tweety begins shooting at the Sylvester-Indians, all the while singing "Ten Little Indians," much the same as in "Scalp Trouble." Another Sylvester-Indian almost captures Tweety, who shouts "Granny, help! A Mohican got me!" Granny rescues Tweety and then they escape the fort and the Sylvester-Indians by disguising themselves as Native Americans.

The depictions of Native Americans conformed to long-established patterns. The fierce warrior and the clueless, bumbling Indian were the two most obvious archetypes. In addition, the name calling done by prominent characters such as Porky and Granny—"Injun," "Mohicans," "Redskins"—all represented common epithets for native peoples. The drinking, gullibility, and the marking off of Native American dead, as if their lives even in cartoon form were meaningless, all signaled the racist perceptions that many white Americans had of Native Americans and that these shorts exploited.

A number of other companies also attempted to censor some of their most racist cartoons. The original *Popeye* shorts, for example, frequently contained material considered offensive in the decades after World War II. *Popeye*, originally developed by Elzie Segar as a newspaper comic strip, became a cartoon character under Max Fleischer's oversight. The racism that ran through the very first *Popeye* cartoon, which was part of a *Betty Boop* short titled simply "Popeye the Sailor" (1933), involved Popeye defending Olive Oyl from Bluto, an unnaturally large character who was also known as "Brutus." In an unrelated scene, Bluto and Popeye test each other's strength in a "ball toss" game. The target of the game is a bobbing head, which happened to be the caricatured head of a black person. The head has large bright lips, dark skin, large white eyes, and bushy hair. He is hit by balls several times but seems to experience no pain. In the next scene, a monkey-like figure, who also approximates some African features, announces a hula dancer named Betty Boop. Betty seems to be somewhat ethnicized herself, perhaps to approximate a Polynesian woman. Her skin is dark brown and she is there to do a fairly risqué hula performance.

Other *Popeye* shorts featured similar racial depictions. In "My Artistical Temperature" (1937) Popeye and Bluto are in an art studio and each turns the other's work of art into a blackface representation. Bluto splashes black paint on Popeye's statue; for Bluto's painting, a landscape with a bright sun, Popeye squirts black paint onto the sun. The blackface sun character comes to life and says "Mammy" before setting. In addition to these stereotypical portrayals, Popeye battles the Japanese. Because he depicts a sailor, many of these shorts involved the navy. In the first of these anti-Japanese episodes, "The Mighty Navy" (1941), Popeye almost singlehandedly defeats the Japanese Navy.[31] No actual Japanese sailors are depicted; instead, the animators made the ships appear Japanese-like and stereotypical-sounding music plays in the background.

The most famous wartime Popeye cartoon was "You're a Sap, Mr. Jap" (1942). In this short, Popeye discovers a Japanese ship with several highly caricatured yellowface sailors on board. The two main characters, who appear to be identical, have huge buck teeth, wear glasses, have "slanted" eyes, wear long robes and wooden geta, and speak in a Japanese-sounding gibberish. Popeye defeats them, but soon their small ship rises from the sea and is in fact a very large ship. Popeye then takes on and defeats the sailors on this larger ship, all of whom are yellowface but unlike the original two sailors they are diminutive. The Japanese commander, who has "lost face," commits suicide by drinking gasoline and swallowing firecrackers. As his boat sinks, the sound of a toilet flushing marks the ship's demise as the song "You're a sap, sap, sap Mr. Jap" is sung in the background.

Popeye's antics against the Japanese, and the Germans as well, appear in four other wartime cartoons. These shorts, "Scrap the Japs" (1942) and "Spinach fer Britain," "Seein' Red, White, 'n' Blue," and "A Jolly Good Furlough" (all from 1943), contained the same stock plotlines and racist stereotypes seen in other World War II propaganda cartoons. These include yellowface Japanese soldiers or sailors who are almost always buffoonish and incompetent and who speak broken English or a Japanese-like gibberish. These types of shorts differ slightly from blackface or redface cartoons in that they came out of war era expediencies designed to demonize the enemy. However, the racist aspects of these cartoons do not differ markedly from others, including other forms of yellowface, and their goal, much like other racial depictions, was either to instruct audiences as to how they should regard nonwhite people or to reinforce preexisting racial prejudices.

Popeye cartoons of the 1940s also displayed grotesque depictions of African Americans. In "Wotta Knight" (1947), produced in color, Popeye and Bluto joust as a royal official keeps score. He also marks time in the joust by ringing a bell held by a pickaninny-type figure. In another scene, Bluto describes himself as the "Black Knight" shortly before getting sprayed with soot from a chimney, which renders him in blackface. Two other episodes utilize indigenous, African-looking blackface individuals reminiscent of those in "His Mouse Friday" and other shorts. In these episodes, "Pop-Pie a la Mode" (1945) and "Island Fling" (1946), the natives all speak like American blacks, rendering them both island cannibals and recognizable blackface Stepin Fetchits. In the first, Popeye is stranded on a raft as a big-lipped blackface individual paddles quickly by with an advertisement noting that one could find assistance at Joe's Inn. Popeye hightails it to Joe's, where a very large blackface individual, presumably "Joe," with big lips, a vest with no shirt, and a small black top hat with a bone through it, spies on Popeye and states in a deep, raspy voice, "Ah, dere's a man of mah tastes." Joe is next seen with a book on "how to serve your fellow man" by one "Ima Cannibal." Then a group of cannibals, playing tom-tom drums, plan to eat Popeye. He finally gets his spinach, defeats the natives, and assumes Joe's position as leader.

In "Island Fling," the animators draw on Daniel Defoe's *Robinson Crusoe* (1719) for inspiration to render a blackface character, "Friday," who has a bone tied in his hair, sings about serving "Robinson Crusoe" (i.e., Bluto).[32] It turns out Friday and Bluto have been trapped on a deserted island. Friday spots a raft and calls Bluto, yelling, "Hey baws, hey baws," and noting the raft, which contains Popeye and Olive Oyl. Bluto sets out to woo Olive. He and Friday get into a makeshift car; Friday wears a hat indicating he is the chauffeur. Bluto, as in just about every *Popeye* short, attempts to acquire Olive, but fails. In the end, Popeye and Olive escape on a raft. Friday has stowed away, along with a whole family of blackface, native, pickaninnies identified as "Saturday, Sunday, and Monday."

Popeye lampooned numerous other ethnic communities. Like many of the shorts from this period, many producers, distributors, and television networks stopped showing them in the 1960s. Their racist impact, however, remained. The *Popeye* series borrowed heavily from other cartoons, especially in its depictions of black people and, later, Asians. The blackface pickaninnies, often with bones tied in their hair and wearing only loin cloths, represented a timeworn portrayal of nonwhite people as savage and uncivilized. They are either cannibals or servants, most often with dark skin and big, oversized lips. The yellowface also mocked the physical appearance as well as the intelligence and fighting acumen of Japanese people. In all these cases, racial stereotypes connected the world of animation to the very real world of racial persecution and discrimination in American society.

As with many of the *Popeye* shorts, the original *Speedy Gonzales* episodes have also been banned. Robert McKimson created the Speedy Gonzales character in the early 1950s. Later, none other than Friz Freleng redesigned Speedy as the cartoon mouse most people became familiar with. The *Speedy Gonzales* series serves as one of the only cartoon series to feature a title character who caricatured an entire ethno-national community. The series, and Speedy himself, mocked the Mexican/Mexican American community in innumerable ways, both small and large, throughout the series.

Speedy Gonzales originally appeared in a *Merrie Melodies* short entitled "Cat-Tails for Two." The purpose of this short is slightly unclear: director McKimson could have developed the short to introduce two new cat characters, Benny and George, derivative of *Of Mice and Men*'s Lennie and George, or McKimson was purposefully developing a new mouse character, Speedy Gonzales, who only appears a third of the way into "Cat-Tails for Two." Whatever McKimson's motivation, there are Mexican stereotypes that pervade this short and Speedy was the character that audiences were drawn to. The cartoon begins with Benny and George trying to find food. George notices a ship that should be full of mice, because it is a Mexican ship. So George asks, "You like Mexican food?" Benny replies, "Oh yes I do George, it gives me the heartburn and I love it!" So, the first cultural stereotyping in the series relies on an old joke about Mexican food being spicy and causing heartburn. The name of the ship itself ridicules Mexican history: *S.S. Pancho Cucaracha*. In the United States, Mexicans were often demeaned as cockroaches. The famous ditty "La Cucaracha" also came from the Mexican Revolution and may well have referred to Pancho Villa's carriage, which frequently broke down.[33] Hence, the linkage of Pancho Villa and Cucaracha in the ship's title implied a dirty, insect-filled vessel that perhaps was often broken.

George and Benny enter the ship to trap some mice. They bait a large trap before a streak of dust appears, yelling "arriba arriba, yeehaw, andele andele, hola hola andele arriba yeehaw arriba arriba andele andele." In his usage, this phrase probably best translates as Speedy saying, "Come on come on, yeehaw, hurry hurry." Speedy's Spanish is a patois of English and Spanish, and the Spanish part, at least the "arriba" line, is essentially meaningless in Mexican Spanish. His accent is an over-the-top, exaggerated Mexican accent. When he stops long enough for us to get a good look at Speedy, the caricature of Mexicans/Latinos is complete. He appears in a long red shirt, has a greasy-looking head of black hair, and has overly large teeth, one of which is gold. He leaves behind a card that notes he is "Speedy Gonzales, fastest mouse in all Mexico." The remainder of the episode features Speedy outwitting the two cats until they finally give up.

Much of the characteristics of the original Speedy remained in the revised Freleng version of the character, and much of the stereotyping prominent in the series originated with McKimson's Speedy. This included a lampooning of Mexican cultural and historical traditions, as well as the overly exaggerated Mexican accent, his gold buck teeth, and use of Spanglish. Speedy, of course, was not a totally negative representation of Latinos as he is clever and outwits the two cats. Freleng's version changed the character in appearance. Speedy loses his gold buck teeth and red shirt but retains his exaggerated accent and Spanglish. Speedy now wears a white pantsuit combination that seems to reflect a popular style of dress in Vera Cruz. He also wears a bright yellow sombrero and has a red sash around his waist, although he retains his greasy locks. It took three years for Speedy to appear in another cartoon, this one appropriately titled "Speedy Gonzales" (1955).

"Speedy Gonzales" opens with a popular stereotype while the title and credits roll (before the cartoon actually starts). The title scene introduces "Speedy Gonzales" as a sombrero-wearing mouse wrapped in a bright serape and napping under a cactus. The short begins with a group of mice, who seem to speak a Spanish-sounding mix of Portuguese, Spanish, and English. They stand at a fence waiting for an opportunity to steal cheese from a cheese factory guarded by Sylvester the Cat. They always fail, so they call on Speedy to secure the cheese. Speedy is at that moment a kind of circus performer, dodging bullets in a game in which paying customers can attempt to "hit Speedy, win beeg prize." Of course they are never able to hit him. Speedy arrives to help the mice. Shouting his trademark "arriba, andele" line, Speedy races past Sylvester and gets the cheese. He tells the assembled mice, "Dere is plentee more where dis cheese it come from." Speedy then outwits the cat and steals much more cheese.

This type of stereotyping continues in other *Speedy Gonzales* cartoons. The next short, "Tabasco Road" (1957), opens with Speedy performing the Mexican hat dance at a bar. Most of his friends, especially Pablo and Fernando, are drunk, a classic depiction of the borracho in mouse form. After the bar closes, Speedy goes to find his friends, only to be told by another mouse that the two were "muy plenty steenko borracho." Pablo and Fernando encounter a large cat and challenge him to fight. After many back-and-forth scenes of Speedy rescuing his friends from the cat, the cat flees town, passing a "ceety leemits" sign. In "Mexicali Shmoes" (1959) the scenario is altered slightly, for in this short the cats are the drunk, sombrero-wearing Mexicans. In numerous episodes, Speedy is the hero of his mouse friends. In "Gonzales Tamales" (1957), however, Speedy has become a menace to his friends. They hire Sylvester, "the gringo pussy cat," to chase Speedy out of town. Why? According to mouse Pedro, "All de preety girls in love wid Speedy Gonzales, what's left are Chihuahuas." Sylvester, of course, fails, leaving the male mice with nothing more to do than continue lounging with their sombreros pulled down over their faces. "Tortilla Flaps" (1958) continues with this type of racism and chauvinism. A group of mice stand around discussing Speedy. One notes, "You know dis Speedy Gonzales?" to which another mouse responds, "Sí, he go stedy weeth ma seester." Another mouse chimes in, "Speedy Gonzales go stedy with everybody seester."

Speedy Gonzales is clearly replete with ethnic stereotypes. For his part, Speedy is resourceful, cunning, and always able to outwit his opponents. His speaking pattern, dress, and the scenarios he is placed in mark him as the caricature of Mexicans/Mexican Americans/Latinos that he is. But he at least has some redeeming qualities. Many of his associates do not. It is through the other mice and occasionally the Mexicanified cats that we see most clearly the stereotypical elements at work in the series. The other mice and the Mexican cats are all lazy, heavy drinking, and in many cases drunk, lounging, thieving, sombrero wearing, dirty, and stupid. They seem to care only for booze, women, and cheese. They in some episodes turn on their hero because he is taking all the women. They avoid labor of all forms, unless it involves finding alcohol, girls, or cheese. They often live in the trash, converting "el steenko sardinas" tins into shanty homes. The mice at the fence in the original "Speedy Gonzales" are really the "illegal immigrants" of American lore. The fence is in fact the border (if you watch the short you'll notice that the fence stretches off into infinity, in other words it doesn't surround the cheese factory). Thus the mice, and Speedy himself, are unauthorized border crossers who raid the cheese factory because they are moochers who seek only to take the bounties on the other side of the fence.[34]

Conclusion

Speedy Gonzales, Tom and Jerry, Popeye, The Alice Comedies, Felix the Cat, and the Censored Eleven were the animated series titans of the early to mid-twentieth century. These cartoons, and numerous others like them, offered Americans and audiences the world over a novel, cheap form of amusing entertainment. They also offered those audiences important lessons on race. Of all these series, and numerous others like them, there were relatively few positive portrayals of racial and ethnic minorities. Instead, communities of color were lambasted as silly, inferior, odd looking, odd speaking, funny, clownish, prone to drunkenness and gambling, lazy, and stupid. One could not go to a different movie theater or flip to a different channel to find an alternate depiction of people of color because no such depiction or channel existed. These cartoons came from the people who produced them and mirrored societal and personal prejudices, and it has become almost standard to excuse the creations of a Hanna and Barbera, Freleng, Clampett, Avery, Messmer, Disney, or Fleischer because they came from a more racist period in American history. That rationale is weak considering the work of the National Association for the Advancement of Colored People or the Society of American Indians to protest such racism in the popular media was anything but a secret to Hollywood's elite.[35] As the architects of racist and chauvinistic depictions, these men made racism seem natural to generations of Americans.

However, not all Americans appreciated their depictions. There is a reason why the Censored Eleven were banned, a reason why other cartoons were banished, and a reason why that censorship came in the 1960s. The reason, as our Conclusion reveals, lay in the fact that communities of color began to rebel against their portrayals in the popular media. As civil rights movements swept the nation, blacks, Mexican Americans and other Latinos, Native Americans, and Asian Americans all struggled to curb racist depictions in cartoons, movies, advertising, and other forms of popular media.

Conclusion

Racism punctuated the nineteenth- and twentieth-century (and often the twenty-first-century media as well) popular media. The media as an institution drew heavily on racially charged images and ideas because those ideas and images helped sell products. For many years, we believe, not only was the institution plagued by racism, but racism became institutionalized within the industry, to the point that with, say, an ad campaign the obvious choice for a printed flyer or a magazine ad or a movie advert or a television commercial was a racial, nay racist, subject. Put simply, the American popular media for generations was a racist enterprise.

Like numerous other institutions, the racism endemic in the popular media has dissipated to a great extent. Ad executives or movie producers or cartoonists do not today usually pick the most racially charged language or concepts for their products or shows. It seems unlikely, for instance, that a new Parker Brothers card game called "The Game of Ten Little Niggers" would pass muster today. It's doubtful whether a big-budget Hollywood film called *The Greaser* would get the green light today. A new cartoon featuring a wisecracking, brightly dressed, rotund, dark black Mammy-type character most likely would not see the light of day in the current mass media.

It may be tempting to believe that the media wisely altered its own racism. Changing times, one might argue, meant that the media changed as well. If racism was no longer acceptable, or at least it is not as acceptable as it was 50 years ago, then perhaps it makes sense that the media altered its practices. We wish to make two points in this conclusion to complicate this viewpoint. The first point is that without the influence of the African American, Latino/Latina, Asian American, and Native American civil rights struggles, it seems unlikely that the media would have changed as much as it has. This is to say that members of ethno-racial communities and their allies forced moviemakers and cartoonists and ad execs to change their racist practices and eliminate the virulent racism within the industry. Our second point is that while change has certainly been made, there remains work to be done. If racism had totally been banished from the popular media, there would be no movement today to rename a sports team such as the Washington Redskins. Tobacco products also still utilize indigenous people to sell products, such as Redman Tobacco. The buffoonish, ignorant, slow-witted Sambo-type character still makes it into Hollywood films. Latinas can still be utilized in ads as "hot" or highly sexualized—for instance, Tecate Beer a few years back featured an ad with the caption "finally, a cold Latina." Newman's Own Inc. recently developed a highly unpopular "salsa con queso" condiment. The packaging featured the usual mug of Paul Newman, albeit this time he's in brownface, wearing a sombrero and sporting a wispy mustache (one wonders why he lacks the gold tooth). Asians can still be caricatured as wily, possessing secret "Oriental" abilities (Mr. Miyagi, anyone?) or as laundry workers (such as Abercrombie and Fitch's "Wong Brothers Laundry Service" shirts—"two Wongs can make it white!"). To put it simply, while the popular media has made great strides in eliminating racist content, different forms of racism persist in popular media.

People of color had resisted racism in the media for many years. Community and political leaders in groups such as the National Association for the Advancement of Colored People (NAACP) did not sit idly as Hollywood filmmakers ridiculed the people they represented. The NAACP, for example, developed a proud tradition of protesting the racist representation of African Americans in movies. Starting with D. W. Griffith's *Birth of a Nation* (1915), the NAACP challenged the racism and historical misrepresentations of such films by coordinating national protest movements.[1] Alternatively, Native American activists and scholars at the end of the twentieth and beginning of the twenty-first centuries looked back over a century of Hollywood's representation of indigenous Americans and concluded that filmmakers played a role as "co-conspirators" with other cultural and political institutions in the United States in committing "cultural genocide" against Native peoples. Filmmakers engaged in acts of "cultural genocide" by presenting moviegoers with "generic Indian" characters—typically a Planes warrior and either the "nagging squaw drudge" or the hypersexualized "squaw princess." As a result, these overly determined representations effaced the ethnic and linguistic diversity of Native America.[2]

In the 1930s the federal government mandated a level of scrutiny in Hollywood with the Motion Picture Production Code. As we noted in Chapter 3, Pre-Code films could get away with highly sexualized or violent plot themes. The Code was designed to remove this kind of offensive or immoral material, particularly nudity and extreme violence. The advent of the

Production Code Administration (PCA), the group of censors who oversaw films and decided if they could be shown to the American public, furthered the policy teeth of the Code. The precursor of today's rating system, the PCA exercised considerable influence over motion pictures. Alas, many, if not most, of the censors saw nothing wrong with racially offensive material. Indeed, blackface, yellowface, brownface, and redface depictions helped the motion picture industry flourish.[3] Keep in mind that some of Hollywood's most prolific early stars, such as Anna May Wong, fled the industry because of the rampant racism and limited roles in the movie industry. Wong's decision to leave, we would suggest, is a form of protest that demonstrates that not all minorities chose to willingly accept silver screen racism.

Various media enterprises now have screening boards that operate like censors, which means that much of the racist content that might have been acceptable in the nineteenth or twentieth centuries never sees the light of day today. Some examples of racially insensitive media have been updated and sanitized for twenty-first-century audiences. Both Quaker and Mars, the owners of Aunt Jemima and Uncle Ben, respectively, have softened product images of these famous characters. Today, Aunt Jemima appears as a modern, un-mammy-like black woman, not the corporate mammy she was only a few decades back. Uncle Ben, for his part, appears as he did when first created. He did not stereotype black people via his visage, but rather by his name. Today both Aunt Jemima's and Uncle Ben's advertisements rarely use black actors to portray either icon, preferring instead, much as they did in the 1960s, to feature happy white families. Both Aunt Jemima and Uncle Ben appear less racist (or not offensive at all) to many Americans than they did in the early twentieth century. It should be noted that numerous other racist advertisements and their logos or icons have simply disappeared, with companies going out of business or changing their logos to fit the changing times.

In a similar way, popular cartoons of the early to mid-twentieth century have been edited or revised to remove overtly racist imagery. Mammy Two Shoes in *Tom and Jerry* rarely makes an appearance today, as the networks that still show *Tom and Jerry* generally avoid showing episodes in which she appears. In some shorts her moments on screen have simply been deleted, leaving odd gaps in the cartoon episode. In more recent episodes Mammy Two Shoes has been replaced by a thin, white woman, known as "Mrs. Two Shoes" (an interesting name considering the honorific "Mrs.," which would never have been used for a black character). Similarly, the classic "Two Little

Indians" is rarely shown on television. "His Mouse Friday," in which Jerry blackens his face and speaks in gibberish, has effectively been banned from U.S. television because of its racist content. In other instances, the show has been edited to remove offensive imagery. For example, in some episodes both Tom and Jerry get blown up by certain explosive devices that leaves them in blackface. Such images usually only last a second or so and were thus easy for present-day animators to remove, eliminating the racist content.

In a recent DVD release of several classic *Tom and Jerry* episodes, actress Whoopi Goldberg offers an important preamble on the show and notes that it "comes to us from a time when racial and ethnic differences were caricatured in the name of entertainment … revealing society's unfair and hurtful representations of people of color, women, and ethnic groups." Goldberg goes on to castigate animators for these depictions—"These prejudices were wrong then and they are certainly wrong today," she notes. But Goldberg also goes on to note that removing Mammy Two Shoes would be "like pretending she never existed."[4] Whoopi Goldberg's introduction to *Tom and Jerry* is fairly accurate and pointed in its criticisms. For such an introduction to the cartoon, an even more forceful, analytical discussion of Mammy Two Shoes and the long history of racial caricaturing evident in the Mammy archetype would seem to us to be warranted.

Where Mammy Two Shoes or those moments of blackface or redface humor in *Tom and Jerry* and other cartoons have been revised, other cartoons are simply no longer shown. There is a reason why the "Censored Eleven" are known as the "Censored Eleven"—their content was so extreme and grotesque in its racism that United Artists withheld these shorts from syndication, effectively banning their exhibition on television. Many of the other banned cartoons, from the offensive *Popeye* and *Porky Pig* shorts to the *Bugs Bunny* anti-Japanese cartoons, are simply no longer aired. Other cartoons were restricted either by their parent companies or by television stations. *Speedy Gonzales*, for example, as a whole, is no longer shown on any network because of its offensive content.

Where some networks chose not to air racist cartoons, or some advertisers chose to soften or revise their racist logos, in other cases a more forceful response was necessary to convince media executives to alter their racist practices. Such was the case with Frito-Lay's Frito Bandito character. The Bandito's appearance coincided with the heyday of the Chicano movement, the Mexican American struggle for civil rights. Mexican Americans, who had for generations disliked the "border bandit" and "greaser" stereotypes, rose up in protest against Frito-Lay.

The organized Chicano response to the Frito Bandito ad campaign began in San Antonio, Texas, in 1968. That year, a new group called Involvement of Mexican-Americans in Gainful Endeavors (IMAGE) was organized. Longtime local activist Albert Peña Jr. had helped form the group, giving it a radical edge as well as a voice of leadership—Peña had served for many years as the San Antonio (Bexar) County Commissioner. Another group, situated in Washington, D.C., the National Mexican-American Anti-Defamation Committee (NMAADC), was formed to appeal to leaders in the U.S. government and to executives at Frito-Lay. These groups responded negatively to the stereotyping of Mexican-origin people. They initiated a public boycott of Fritos and also appealed to Frito-Lay to remove the Frito Bandito.[5]

Albert Peña was an obvious leader in the anti-Frito Bandito campaign, having previously worked to boycott Bill Dana's "Jose Jimenez" character. That character, like many we have discussed, parodied Mexican-origin people. Dana, whose Jimenez character had a recurring role on *The Steve Allen Show*, mocked Mexican Americans by speaking English poorly with a thick accent and by mispronouncing certain phrases. He opened many of his bits by introducing himself by saying "my name Jose Jimenez" in overly accented fashion (the Jimenez comes out slowly as "he-man-ez"). He also did a Southwestern Bell advertisement hawking their "jellow pages." Many Mexican Americans came to dislike his performances, and Peña helped organize a local boycott in San Antonio. Peña spoke for many when he noted that he used to laugh at such characters until he "realized I was laughing at myself and all Mexican-Americans." He further noted, quite accurately, that "Jose Jimenez and people like him, who insult our heritage and our dignity, are the Stepin Fetchits of the Mexican-American community. And they must go."[6]

Peña was correct, and Bill Dana himself chose to retire the Jimenez character. Actually, Dana went further than that. He terminated his lucrative contract with Southwestern Bell. He publicly denounced the Jimenez character to a crowd of approximately 10,000 Latinos, declaring "Jose Jimenez is dead." He also founded a group entitled Mexican Americans for United Direction, an advocacy organization that, like IMAGE, attempted to challenge negative perception of Mexican Americans.[7] Dana evidently saw the error in his ways, the hurtfulness of his character, chose to admit his mistake, and, more importantly, strove to make sure that others didn't produce similar caricatures.

Frito-Lay chose a different path. First, it denied the hurtfulness of the Frito Bandito character. When protests continued, it attempted to prove that Mexican Americans themselves approved of the character. It did this by generating a selective study that revealed that a majority of Mexican Americans liked the character. When that failed to appease groups like IMAGE, Frito-Lay attempted to tone down the Bandito's most obvious racist attributes: he lost his gold tooth and pistols. This all proved to be less than sufficient for groups such as IMAGE and the NMAADC.

Peña continued his critique of the Frito Bandito, noting, "In the mass media we see Mexican Americans pictured as the Frito Bandito—who steals a package of corn chips and then sneaks off to lay in the sun and drink tequila." Peña turned the Frito Bandito character on its head when he stated, "The real culprit is not the sneaky bandido ... the real sinverguenza [shameless one] is the Frito Lay Co., first they pilfer the frito from the Mexican kitchen ... not satisfied with this, they caricaturize the Mexicano to sell their product." Peña gave voice not only to Mexican American anger over the Bandito character, but also the cultural and cuisine appropriation that were Frito's Corn Chips. He also placed the Bandito, Jose Jimenez, and other characters in context, arguing that Mexican-descent people were more than the "sneaky, thieving rat or a dull-witted[,] lazy, mixed up funny man who speaks broken English."[8] IMAGE went further, developing a list of positive Mexican/Mexican American characters that the media could utilize to move away from negative depictions like the Bandito. These included the "Mexican Vaquero," the "Mexican-American soldier," and the Mexican American "law enforcement image."[9]

It took many years, but Frito-Lay eventually retired the Frito Bandito, replacing him with a group of cowboys known as the "Muncha Bunch." Put simply, the Frito Bandito made Frito-Lay a lot of money, and so it was reluctant to give him up. In fact, a monetary threat proved the straw that broke the camel's back, as the NMAADC filed a $610 million defamation suit against the company. Shortly thereafter, the Bandito was no more. As the *Texas Monthly* observed, "The Frito Bandito has stolen his last chip."[10]

Like the Mexican American community and the Frito Bandito, the use of racial clichés and cultural stereotypes to represent Native Americans in various media formats has transcended the twentieth century and remained a part of American popular culture in the twenty-first century. Both professional and collegiate sports have proven fertile ground for the use of racist mascots. Collegiate athletic teams such as the Florida State University "Seminoles" routinely receive national television coverage, just as the University of Illinois's former mascot, the fictitious Chief Illinwek, did before it was retired in 2007. In professional sports, teams such as the Atlanta Braves, Cleveland Indians, Golden State Warriors, Seattle Seahawks, Kansas City Chiefs, and Chicago Blackhawks continue an inglorious American tradition of trivializing rich Native American traditions and representing indigenous people as mere caricatures.

Most prominently, efforts by Native American groups and their white allies to abolish the "Redskin" mascot from Washington's NFL team has garnered impassioned, and in some cases, racist, responses. Responding to the accusations of team supporters and staff that opposition to the Redskin mascot is a form of "political correctness," Native American studies scholar Steven Salaita observes:

> Redskin. The word relegates complex humanity to a lifeless specimen, a stagnant and specious simulation of a physiognomy invented during a time of conquest. It reduces cultural identity to the wholly unreliable tableau of melanin and nose structure. It is of a specific historical moment, but exists outside of time, like the immutable figure it purports to represent.
>
> The mascot accompanying the word is a brand, a commodity, selling not merely image or design but also the thoroughgoing cant of colonial fantasy. It also sells identity. The identity it peddles has nothing to do with being Native.[11]

Salaita's observations touch on how pop culture representations of Native American people perpetuate a relationship between indigenous and non-indigenous people grounded in the enduring reality of colonialism in the United States. The complexities of Native American life and culture are therefore lost in this continuing creation of a fictive "Indian" that white Americans invented and disingenuously ordained as "authentic."

The Washington Redskins began life in the early 1930s as the Boston Braves football team. George Preston Marshall—a man known for his reactionary political views, racism, and for being a "tightwad"—owned the Boston Braves. The Braves were coached by Will "Lone Star" Dietz, a Native American and former athlete himself. Dietz began his life in American football at the Carlisle Indian School, where he was a player. He subsequently coached a number of college football teams, including the Native American industrial training school, the Haskell Institute. It was from this position that Marshall hired Dietz to coach the Boston Braves. According to Marshall's granddaughter, Jordan Harrison Price's story, George Preston Marshall nicknamed the team the Redskins after he moved the franchise to Washington, D.C. The name was allegedly chosen in honor of Dietz, but for a team that became associated with the South during the era of Jim Crow, Marshall clearly saw the marketing opportunities that would open to him by naming his team the Redskins.

It is far too glib, and ahistorical, to suggest that the use of Native American mascots was in keeping with the cultural tenor of the times. Long before Marshall began using the Redskin mascot, Native American leaders derided the use of that word as racially offensive. For example, early twentieth-century Native American organizations such as the Society of American Indians (SAI), led efforts to eradicate racist depictions of indigenous people in American culture. SAI leaders such as Arthur C. Parker (Seneca Nation), Charles Eastman (Santee-Sioux), Carlos Montezuma (Mohave-Apache), Sherman Coolidge (Arapaho), Howard E. Gansworth (Tuscarora), Henry Roe Cloud (Winnebago), and John M. Oskison (Cherokee) strove to instill Native Americans with "race pride." One of the ways that attempted to instill such pride was by actively resisting the caricaturing of Native Americans with terms such as "squaw" and "redskin," by attacking racist stereotypes in Buffalo Bill Cody's Wild West performances, and by openly mocking the efforts of wealthy Americans, such as department store millionaire Rodman Wanamaker, who wanted to erect a National American Indian Memorial on Staten Island at the entrance to New York Harbor. As Sherman Coolidge quipped in response to Wanamaker's scheme: "They [Native Americans] do not need that memorial. The Indian is not dead. He is very much alive, and needs greater things than statues."[12]

Native American protests over the use of offensive sports mascots like the "Redskins" continued into the late twentieth century. During the 1970s, for instance, the American Indian Movement led indigenous efforts to rid the pop culture landscape of racist mascots.[13] More recently, the Oneida Indian Nation has led the "Change the Mascot" campaign, a coordinated effort to raise public awareness about the offensiveness of the Redskin mascot and to abolish it from professional sports.[14] Such efforts have been met with a concerted public relations campaign from the Washington Redskins' organization, which claim the mascot is "tradition" and "honors" Native peoples.[15]

Current Washington Redskins owner Dan Snyder, who has vowed "NEVER" to change the team name, takes the position that the mascot is a source of pride and tradition. This may be true for white and black

Americans who don war paint, wear team clothing, and support the Washington football team, but social science research is unequivocal in pointing to the harm that such popular emblems cause indigenous people, especially children. Supporters of the Washington Redskin football team insist that there are larger "problems" confronting Native Americans than a sports team's mascot. What such critics miss is how issues of cultural representation and socioeconomic opportunity are tied. One study found that children and adults who are exposed to "stereotypical cultural beliefs about all Indians living in tipis, being warlike, migratory hunters, carrying tomahawks, carving totem poles, and speaking 'Indian' in cartoons, TV shows, and movies" tend to exhibit lower self-esteem, and as a result have lower life expectations.[16] For the corporate interests and marketing agencies invested in promoting (and making money from) professional sports franchises like the Washington Redskins, such considerations appear inconsequential to their business models.

The debate over sports mascots as a form of racist popular media is ongoing and, at this stage, how this issue will resolve is a matter of conjecture. Will teams such as the Redskins follow the Bill Dana route, or the Frito Bandito route, or something else entirely? What seems most clear from this debate is that the issue of race and racism in the popular media remains a problem within the mass media and the entertainment and sports industries today.

Racism in American Popular Media has attempted to shed light on the multifaceted ways in which racism has become embedded and institutionalized in the American popular media. Much of the American popular media originated in the "racial century"—that period between 1850 and 1950 during which racist views were societally acceptable—and as such it is perhaps not surprising that advertisers and cartoonist and moviemakers and writers would utilize racist imagery and ideas. Many of those racist archetypes used by the media have fallen by the wayside, as has in many cases the racism that ran through racist stereotyping and caricaturing. But problems remain. The history of media racism should not be forgotten or swept under the rug simply because times have changed. A better understanding of that history may well help destroy the vestiges of racism that remain with the media today.

Notes

Introduction

1. LeRoy Ashby, *With Amusement for All: A History of American Popular Culture since 1830* (Revised Edition, Lexington: University of Kentucky Press, 2012), xv–xvi.

2. Television programs may seem an obvious omission to our discussion. Television came late to the world of popular media, and the advent of network censors ensured that the most virulent forms of racism rarely made it into people's homes. The world of television tended to be a white and conservative one, with few programs focusing on people of color before the late 1960s, and the omission of nonwhites can certainly be interpreted as racist. It is also true that popular Westerns, for instance, contained many of the same racist archetypes we describe in this book. But those images originated in other forms of media and were transferred to the small screen. Therefore, we do not focus sustained attention on racism in the television industry.

3. Polly E. McLean, "Mass Communication, Popular Culture, and Racism" in *Racism and Anti-Racism in World Perspective*, ed. Benjamin P. Bowser (Thousand Oaks, CA: Sage Publications, 1995), 85; Carla D. Hunter and Ma'at E. Lewis-Coles, "Coping with Racism: A Spirit-Based Psychological Perspective" in *Racism in America: The Psychology of Prejudice and Discrimination*, ed. Jean Lau Chin (Westport, CT: Praeger, 2004), 209.

4. Clyde Taylor, "The Re-Birth of the Aesthetic in Cinema" in *The Birth of Whiteness: Race and the Emergence of U.S. Cinema*, ed. Daniel Bernardi (New Brunswick, NJ: Rutgers University Press, 1996), 17.

5. R. Kent Weaver and Bert A. Rockman, "Assessing the Effects of Institutions," in *Do Institutions Matter? Government Capabilities in the United States and Abroad*, eds. R. Kent Weaver and Bert A. Rockman (Washington, DC: The Brookings Institution, 1993), 4–8; Karol Soltan, "Institutions as Products of Politics" in *Institutions and Social Order*, eds. Karol Soltan, Eric M. Uslaner, and Virginia Haufler (Ann Arbor: University of Michigan Press, 1998), 46–47.

6. Lawrence Grossberg, Ellen Wartella, D. Charles Whitney, and J. MacGregor Wise, *Media Making: Mass Media in a Popular Culture* (Thousand Oaks, CA: Sage Publications, 2006), xx–xxi.

Chapter 1

1. David Murray, "Translation and Mediation" in *The Cambridge Companion to Native American Literature*, eds. Joy Porter and Kenneth M. Roemer (New York: Cambridge University Press, 2005), 71; Gene A. Jarrett, *Representing the Race: A New Political History of African American Literature* (New York: New York University Press, 2011), 74.

2. Kimberly Wallace-Sanders, *Mammy: A Century of Race, Gender, and Southern Memory* (Ann Arbor: University of Michigan Press, 2008), 89, 108; Robert F. Berkhofer Jr., *The White Man's Indian: Images of the American Indian from Columbus to the Present* (New York: Vintage, 1978), 41, 102; Steven Bender, *Greasers and Gringos: Latinos, Law, and the American Imagination* (New York: New York University Press, 2003), 4; Xiao-huang Yin, *Chinese American Literature since the 1850s* (Bloomington: University of Illinois Press, 2000), 138.

3. Susan Currell, "Introduction" in *Popular Eugenics: National Efficiency and American Mass Culture in the 1930s*, eds. Susan Currell and Christina Cogdell (Athens: Ohio University Press, 2006), 1–14; Gregory D. Smithers, *Science, Sexuality, and Race in the United States and Australia, 1780s–1890s* (New York and London: Routledge, 2009), chapter 2.

4. David Brody, *Visualizing American Empire: Orientalism and Imperialism in the Philippines* (Chicago: University of Chicago Press, 2010).

5. Catherine Silk and John Silk, *Racism and Anti-Racism in American Popular Culture: Portrayals of African Americans in Fiction and Film* (Manchester: Manchester University Press, 1990), ix.

6. A. Dirk Moses, "Conceptual Blockages and Definitional Dilemmas in the 'Racial Century': Genocides of Indigenous Peoples and the Holocaust," *Patterns of Prejudice* 36, no. 4 (2002): 7–36.

7. Daniel J. Kelves, *In the Name of Eugenics: Genetics and the Uses of Human Heredity* (Berkeley: University of California Press, 1985); Wendy Kline, *Building a Better Race: Gender, Sexuality, and Eugenics from the Turn of the Century to the Baby Boom* (Berkeley: University of California Press, 2001); Christine Rosen, *Preaching Eugenics: Religious Leaders and the American Eugenics Movement* (New York: Oxford University Press, 2004); Alexandra M. Stern, *Eugenic Nation: Faults and Frontiers for Better Breeding in Modern America* (Berkeley: University of California Press, 2005).

8. Charlotte Perkins Gilman's *Herland* (1915; rpr., New York: Pantheon Books, 1979).

9. Erskine Caldwell, *The Bastard* (1915; rpr., New York: Heron Press, 1929); Dan B. Miller, *Erskine Caldwell: The Journey from Tobacco Road: A Biography* (New York: Alfred A. Knopf, 1995), 107.

10. Madison Grant, *The Passing of the Great Race* (1916; rpr., Abergele, UK: Wermod and Wermod Publishing Group, 2012); Lothrop Stoddard, *The Rising Tide of Color against White World-Supremacy* (New York: Charles Scribner's Sons,

1920). For further analysis, see Jonathon P. Spiro, *Defending the Master Race: Conservation, Eugenics, and the Legacy of Madison Grant* (Lebanon, NH: University of Vermont Press, 2009).

11. Drew Gilpin Faust, *The Ideology of Slavery: Proslavery Thought in the Antebellum South, 1830–1860* (Baton Rouge: Louisiana State University Press, 1981); Larry E. Tise, *Proslavery: A History of the Defense of Slavery in America, 1701–1840* (Athens: University of Georgia Press, 1987); Charles F. Irons, *The Origins of Proslavery Christianity: White and Black Evangelicals in Colonial and Antebellum Virginia* (Chapel Hill: University of North Carolina Press, 2008).

12. Samuel George Morton, *Crania Americana: Or a Comparative View of the Skulls of Various Aboriginal Nations of North and South America* (Philadelphia: J. Dobson, 1839).

13. Ann Fabian, *The Skull Collectors: Race, Science, and Americas Unburied Dead* (Chicago: University of Chicago Press, 2010), 82.

14. Morton, *Crania Americana*, 23–24.

15. William Stanton, *The Leopard's Spots: Scientific Attitudes toward Race in America, 1815–59* (Chicago: University of Chicago Press, 1960).

16. Robert E. Bieder, *Science Encounters the Indian, 1820–1880: The Early Years of American Ethnology* (Norman: University of Oklahoma Press, 1986), 73.

17. Morton, *Crania Americana*, 2.

18. Ibid., 7; Smithers, *Science, Sexuality, and Race*, 49–50.

19. On these and related points, see Stephen Jay Gould, *The Mismeasure of Man* (New York: W.W. Norton and Company, 1981).

20. David Topper, "Towards an Epistemology of Scientific Illustration" in *Picturing Knowledge: Historical and Philosophical Problems Concerning the Use of Art in Science*, ed. Brian S. Baigrie (Toronto: University of Toronto Press, 1996), 232.

21. Morton, *Crania Americana*, 3.

22. Drew Gilpin Faust, *Southern Stories: Slaveholders in Peace and War* (Columbia: University of Missouri Press, 1992), 16–17; David Torbett, *Theology and Slavery: Charles Hodge and Horace Bushnell* (Macon, GA: Mercer University Press, 2006), 20, 31.

23. Thornton Stringfellow, *Scriptural and Statistical Views in Favor of Slavery* (4th edition, Richmond, VA: J.W. Randolph, 1856), 105.

24. Ibid., 70.

25. Quoted in Elizabeth Fox-Genovese and Eugene Genovese, *The Mind of the Master Class: History and Faith in the Southern Slaveholders' Worldview* (New York: Cambridge University Press, 2005), 492.

26. Tise, *Proslavery*, 205; John P. Daly, *When Slavery Was Called Freedom: Evangelicalism, Proslavery, and the Causes of the Civil War* (Lexington: University of Kentucky Press, 2002), 41; James A. Harrill, *Slaves in the New Testament: Literary. Social, and Moral Dimensions* (New York: Augsburg Fortress, 2006), 182; Eran

Shalev, *American Zion: The Old Testament as a Political Text from the Revolution to the Civil War* (New Haven, CT: Yale University Press, 2013), 101.

27. Karen M. Smith, "Southern Women Writers' Responses to *Uncle Tom's Cabin*" in *The History of Southern Women's Literature*, eds. Carolyn Perry and Mary Louise Weaks (Baton Rouge: Louisiana State University Press, 2002), 97–102; Sarah Meer, *Uncle Tom Mania: Slavery, Minstrelsy, and Transatlantic Culture in the 1850s* (Athens: University of Georgia Press, 2005), 75.

28. Josiah Nott and George Gliddon, *Types of Mankind; Or, Ethnological Researches* (7th edition, Philadelphia: Lippincott, Grambo and Co., 1855). For analysis, see Bruce R. Dain, *A Hideous Monster of the Mind: American Race Theory in the Early Republic* (Cambridge, MA: Harvard University Press, 2002); Smithers, *Science, Sexuality, and Race*, chapter 2.

29. See, for example, John Harris, *The Pre-Adamite Earth: Contributions to Theological Science* (Boston: Gould and Lincoln, 1851).

30. Isabella Duncan, *Pre-Adamite Man; or, the Story of Our Old Planet and Its Inhabitants, Told by Scripture and Science* (2nd edition, London: Saunders, Otley, and Co., 1860), v.

31. Colin Kidd, *The Forging of Races: Race and Scripture in the Protestant Atlantic World, 1600–2000* (New York: Cambridge University Press, 2006), 161–62; David N. Livingstone, *Adam's Ancestors: Race, Religion, and the Politics of Human Origins* (Baltimore: Johns Hopkins University Press, 2008), 65–66.

32. Ariel (Buckner Payne), *The Negro: What Is His Ethnological Status* (Cincinnati, self-published by the author, 1867), 21, italics in original.

33. Ibid., 23.

34. Ibid., 44.

35. Ibid., 48.

36. David M. Chalmers, *Backfire: How the Ku Klux Klan Helped the Civil Rights Movement* (Lanham, MD: Rowman and Littlefield Publishers, Inc., 2003), 173.

37. Charles Carroll, *The Negro a Beast: Or, in the Image of God* (1900; rpr., Miami, FL: Mnemosyne Pub. Co., 1969), 44; Fay Botham, *Almighty God Created the Races: Christianity, Interracial Marriage, and American Law* (Chapel Hill: University of North Carolina Press, 2009), 104–5.

38. Carroll, *The Negro a Beast*, 71.

39. Ibid., 80.

40. Ibid., 102.

41. Ibid., 233.

42. Ibid., 228–29.

43. Frances E.W. Harper, *Iola Leroy, or, Shadows Uplifted* (Philadelphia: Garrigues Brothers, 1892), 109. Literary scholars have produced a considerable body of work devoted to interracial marriage, mixed-race identities (especially as it related to "passing"), and antiblack racism. See, for example, Debra J. Rosenthal, *Race Mix-*

ture in Nineteenth-Century U.S. and Spanish American Fictions (Chapel Hill: University of North Carolina Press, 2004); Eve A. Raimon, *The "Tragic Mulatta" Revisited: Race and Nationalism in Nineteenth-Century Antislavery Fiction* (New Brunswick, NJ: Rutgers University Press, 2004); Daniel A. Novak, *Realism, Photography, and Nineteenth-Century Fiction* (New York: Cambridge University Press, 2008).

44. Frederick Douglass, "God Almighty Made but One Race (1884)" in *Race and Liberty in America: The Essential Reader*, ed. Jonathan Bean (Lexington: The University of Kentucky Press, 2009), 97–98.

45. Jean-Jacques Rousseau, *A Discourse on the Origin of Inequality and a Discourse on Political Economy* (Amsterdam: Marc Michel Rey, 1755; translated by G.D.H. Cole, Stilwell, KS, 2005), 29. For further analysis of this point, see Roy Harvey Pearce, *Savagism and Civilization: A Study of the Indian and the American Mind* (1953; rpr., Berkeley: University of California Press, 1988), 99; Bernard Sheehan, *Savagism and Civility: Indians and Englishmen in Colonial Virginia* (New York: Cambridge University Press, 1980), 3; Anthony Pagden, *European Encounters with the New World: From Renaissance to Romanticism* (New Haven, CT: Yale University Press, 1993), 166–68; Karen Ordahl Kupperman, *Indians and English: Facing Off in Early America* (Ithaca, NY: Cornell University Press, 2000), 20.

46. Pearce, *Savagism and Civilization*, 172.

47. Roy Harvey Pearce, *Savagism and Civilization*, 192; David A. Gerstner, *Manly Arts: Masculinity and Nation in Early American Cinema* (Durham, NC: Duke University Press, 2006), 26.

48. Pearce, *Savagism and Civilization*, 147; David A. Gerstner, *Manly Arts: Masculinity and Nation in Early American Cinema* (Durham, NC: Duke University Press, 2006), 26.

49. Ronald A. Bosco and Joel Myerson, eds., *The Later Lectures of Ralph Waldo Emerson, 1843–1871* (volume 2: 1855–1971, Athens: University of Georgia Press, 2001), 58. See also Pearce, *Savagism and Civilization*, 147.

50. Patrick Brantlinger, *Dark Vanishings: Discourses on the Extinction of Primitive Races, 1800–1930* (Ithaca, NY: Cornell University Press, 2003), 6.

51. Nott quoted in Reginald Horsman, *Race and Manifest Destiny: The Origins of American Racial Anglo-Saxonism* (Cambridge, MA: Harvard University Press, 1981), 155.

52. William J. Scheick, *The Half-Blood: A Cultural Symbol in 19th-Century American Fiction* (Lexington: University of Kentucky Press, 1979), 2.

53. Manuel G. Gonzales, *Mexicanos: A History of Mexicans in the United States* (2nd edition, Bloomington: Indiana University Press, 2009), 148.

54. Francisco E. Balderrama and Raymond Rodriguez, *Decade of Betrayal: Mexican Repatriation in the 1930s* (Revised Edition, Albuquerque: University of New Mexico Press, 2006).

55. George Lippard, *Legends of Mexico* (Philadelphia: T.B. Peterson, 1847), 15.

56. Ibid., 47.

57. James W. Parins, *John Rollin Ridge: His Life and Works* (Lincoln: University of Nebraska Press, 2004), 106.

58. Thomas Torrans, *The Magic Curtain: The Mexican-American Border in Fiction, Film, and Song* (Fort Worth: Texas Christian University Press, 2002), 7, 17–19.

59. Will Comfort, *Somewhere South of Sonora* (New York: Houghton Mifflin, 1925).

60. As quoted in Thomas Torrans, *The Magic Curtain: The Mexican-American Border in Fiction, Film, and Song*, 130.

61. J.E. Smyth, *Edna Ferber's Hollywood: American Fictions of Gender, Race, and History* (Austin: University of Texas Press, 2010), 196.

62. Robert Leleux, "Giant Scandal," *Texas Observer*, August 22, 2011.

63. On the "yellow peril" and the "rising tide of color" see John Kuo Wei Tchen and Dylan Yeats, eds., *Yellow Peril!: An Archive of Anti-Asian Fear* (London: Verso, 2014); Stoddard, *The Rising Tide of Color*. On the tortured history of immigration in the United States and its enduring resonance, see John Higham, *Strangers in the Land: Patterns of American Nativism, 1860–1925* (New Brunswick, NJ: Rutgers University Press, 1955); Elmer C. Sandmeyer, *The Anti-Chinese Movement in California* (Bloomington: University of Illinois Press, 1973); Mae M. Ngai, *Impossible Subjects: Illegal Aliens and the Making of Modern America* (Princeton, NJ: Princeton University Press, 2004).

64. Jenny Clegg, *Fu Manchu and the Yellow Peril: The Making of a Racist Myth* (Staffordshire, UK: Trentham Books, 1994); Jachinson Chan, *Chinese American Masculinities: From Fu Manchu to Bruce Lee* (New York and London: Routledge, 2000), chapter 2.

65. Sax Rohmer, *The Insidious Dr. Fu-Manchu: Being a Somewhat Detailed Account of the Amazing Adventures of Nayland Smith in His Trailing the Sinister Chinaman* (New York: McBride, Nast and Company, 1913), 4.

66. Ibid., 25–26.

67. Ibid., 204.

68. Earl Derr Biggers, *The House without a Key* (1925; rpr., Holicong, PA: Wildside Press, 2002).

69. *Simple Addition by a Little Nigger* (New York: McLoughlin Brothers, 1874); Mary H.B. Wade, *Ten Little Indians: Stories of How Indian Children Lived and Played* (Boston: W.A. Wilde Company, 1904); Jan N. Pieterse, *White on Black: Images of Africa and Blacks in Western Popular Culture* (New Haven, CT: Yale University Press, 1995), 166. The English novelist Agatha Christie wrote a play that borrowed from these children's stories. It was entitled *Ten Little Niggers* (London: Samuel French, 1944). For Tintin, see Pierre Assouline, *Herge: The Man Who Created Tintin* (New York: Oxford University Press, 2009).

70. Mark Twain, *The Adventures of Huckleberry Finn* (New York: Harper and Brothers Publishers, 1884). For further analysis, see James S. Leonard, Thomas

A. Tenney, and Thadious M. Davis, eds., *Satire or Evasion? Black Perspectives on Huckleberry Finn* (Durham, NC: Duke University Press, 1999).

71. Laura Ingalls Wilder, *Little House on the Prairie* (New York: Harper and Brothers, 1935), 87.

72. Walt Disney's *Mickey Mouse and the Boy Thursday* (Park Ridge, IL: Whitman, 1948).

73. Ann Folwell Stanford, *Bodies in a Broken World: Women Novelists of Color and the Politics of Medicine* (Chapel Hill: University of North Carolina Press, 2003), 87.

74. Michael Waltman and John Haas, *The Communication of Hate* (New York: Peter Lang Publishing, Inc., 2011), 158.

Chapter 2

1. Maurice M. Manring, *Slave in a Box: The Strange Career of Aunt Jemima* (Charlottesville: University of Virginia Press, 1998), 60–66.

2. Jason Chambers, *Madison Avenue and the Color Line: African Americans in the Advertising Industry* (Philadelphia: University of Pennsylvania Press, 2008), 1.

3. Jackson Lears, *Fables of Abundance: A Cultural History of Advertising in America* (New York: Basic Books, 1994), 1.

4. Benedict Anderson, *Imagined Communities: Reflections on the Origin and Spread of Nationalism* (New York: Verso, 1983), 6; Susan J. Douglas, *Listening In: Radio and the American Imagination* (Minneapolis: University of Minnesota Press, 2004), 157.

5. Lears, *Fables of Abundance*, 3.

6. Anne McClintock, *Imperial Leather: Race, Gender and Sexuality in the Colonial Contest* (New York and London: Routledge, 1995), 32. See also C. Richard King, Carmen R. Lugo-Lugo, and Mary K. Bloodsworth-Lugo, *Animated Difference: Race, Gender, and Sexuality in Contemporary Films for Children* (Lanham, MD: Rowman and Littlefield, 2011), 131.

7. Kristin L. Hoganson, *Consumers' Imperium: The Global Production of American Domesticity, 1865–1920* (Chapel Hill: University of North Carolina Press, 2007), 9, 14.

8. Ibid., 13, 55; John Higham, *Strangers in the Land: Patterns of American Nativism, 1860–1925* (New Brunswick, NJ: Rutgers University Press, 1955); Frank Wu, *Yellow: Race in America beyond Black and White* (New York: Basic Books, 2003).

9. Marilyn Kern-Foxworth, *Aunt Jemima, Uncle Ben, and Rastus: Black in Advertising, Yesterday, Today, and Tomorrow* (Westport, CT: Praeger, 1994), 38–39.

10. Chambers, *Madison Avenue and the Color Line*, 5.

11. Kristina DuRoucher, *Raising Racists: The Socialization of White Children in the Jim Crow South* (Lexington: University of Kentucky Press, 2011), 76.

12. Gary Cross, *Kids' Stuff: Toys and the Changing World of American Childhood* (Cambridge, MA: Harvard University Press, 1997), 99; Jabari Asim, *The N Word: Who Can Say It, Who Shouldn't, and Why* (New York: Houghton Mifflin Company, 2007), 103–4; Anthony J. Stanonis, "Introduction: Selling Dixie" in *Dixie's Emporium: Tourism, Foodways, and Consumer Culture in the American South*, ed. Anthony J. Stanonis (Athens: University of Georgia Press, 2008), 9.

13. Nancy S. Dye, "Introduction" in *Gender, Class, Race, and Reform in the Progressive Era*, eds. Noralee Frankel and Nancy S. Dye (Lawrence: University of Kansas Press, 1991), 1–9.

14. *Pearson's Magazine* 23 (1910): 32. See also Nell Irvin Painter, *Standing at Armageddon: The United States, 1877–1919* (New York: W.W. Norton, 1987), 141–69.

15. Hawkins quoted in *Printers' Ink: A Journal for Advertisers* 46 (July 1911): 68.

16. See http://madvertisementsblog.blogspot.com/2012/06/chlorinol-bleaching-soda.html, accessed August 14, 2014.

17. Ellen G. Spears, *Baptized in PCBs: Race, Pollution, and Justice in an All-American Town* (Chapel Hill: University of North Carolina Press, 2014), 75–76.

18. Diane Roberts, *The Myth of Aunt Jemima: White Women Representing Black Women* (New York and London: Routledge, 2003), 1.

19. Manring, *Slave in a Box*, 2–3, 7.

20. "Our Products," http://www.auntjemima.com/aj_products/, accessed April 12, 2014.

21. LeRoy Ashby, *With Amusement for All: A History of American Popular Culture since 1830* (Lawrence: University of Kentucky Press, 2006), 11, 14–15.

22. Ashby, *With Amusement for All*, 19–21; Debra L. Merskin, *Media, Minorities, and Meaning: A Critical Introduction* (New York: Peter Lang Publishing, 2011), 265–66.

23. Alice A. Deck, " 'Now Then—Who Said Biscuits?' The Black Woman Cook as Fetish in American Advertising, 1905–1953" in *Kitchen Culture in America: Popular Representations of Food, Gender, and Race*, ed. Sherrie A. Inness (Philadelphia: University of Pennsylvania Press, 2001), 69.

24. Manring, *Slave in a Box*, 8.

25. Excerpts from the Aunt Jemima Variety Hour can be found at the Jim Crow Museum, https://www.youtube.com/user/jimcrowmuseum/videos.

26. Kern-Foxworth, *Aunt Jemima, Uncle Ben, and Rastus*, 49; Sherri Liberman, *American Food by the Decades* (Santa Barbara, CA: Greenwood, 2011), 116–17.

27. Kern-Foxworth, *Aunt Jemima, Uncle Ben, and Rastus*, 36.

28. *Life*, September 25, 1950; April 20, 1953, 166.

29. Ronald D. Michman and Edward M. Mazze, *The Food Industry Wars: Marketing Triumphs and Blunders* (Westport, CT: Greenwood Publishing Group, Inc., 1998), 221.

30. Mark Pendergrast, *For God, Country, and Coca-Cola* (New York: Basic Books, 2013).

31. Bob Stoddard, *The Encyclopedia of Pepsi-Cola Collectibles* (Iola, WI: Krause Publications, 2002), 9.

32. Chambers, *Madison Avenue and the Color Line*, 95.

33. Stephanie Capparell, *The Real Pepsi Challenge: The Inspirational Story of Breaking the Color Barr* (New York: Wall Street Journal Books, 2007).

34. Ibid., x; Chambers, *Madison Avenue and the Color Line*, 60–62.

35. Judy Vaknin, *Smoke Signals: 100 Years of Tobacco Advertising* (London: Middlesex University Press, 2007), 57.

36. Klaus Lubbers, *Born in the Shade: Stereotypes of the Native American in United States Literature and the Visual Arts, 1776–1894* (Amsterdam: Rodopi, 1994), 195–96; Joseph C. Winter, "Traditional Uses of Tobacco by Native Americans" in *Tobacco Use by Native Americans: Sacred Smoke and Silent Killer*, ed. Joseph C. Winter (Norman: University of Oklahoma Press, 2000), 32.

37. Robert N. Proctor, *Golden Holocaust: Origins of the Cigarette Catastrophe and the Case for Abolition* (Berkeley: University of California Press, 2011), 175.

38. Russell M. Lawson, *Encyclopedia of American Indian Issues Today* (Santa Barbara, CA: Greenwood, 2013), 64.

39. Gail Guthrie Valaskakis, *Indian Country: Essays on Contemporary Native Culture* (Waterloo: Wilfred Laurier University Press, 2005), 73.

40. Doleres B. Mitchell, "Power and Pleasure in 19th Century Tobacco Art" in *Tobacco and Health*, ed. Karen Slama (New York: Plenum Press, 1995), 921; Rayna Green, "The Pocahontas Perplex: The Image of Indian Women in American Culture" in *Contested Images: Women of Color in Popular Culture*, ed. Alma M. Garcia (Lanham, MD: AltaMira Press, 2012), 162; Lawrence D. Bobo and Mia Tuan, *Prejudice in Politics: Group Position, Public Opinion, and the Wisconsin Treaty Rights Dispute* (Cambridge, MA: Harvard University Press, 2006), 65; Donald Fixico, *Daily Life of Native Americans in the Twentieth Century* (Westport, CT: Greenwood Press, 2006), 171–72.

41. Jim Cox, *Sold on Radio: Advertisers in the Golden Age of Broadcasting* (Jefferson, NC: McFarland and Company, 2008), 114.

42. Joel Pfister, *The Yale Indian: The Education of Henry Roe Cloud* (New Haven, CT: Yale University Press, 2009), 12.

43. By the mid-twentieth century, caricatures of Native American warriors often did not appear in advertisements. For instance, Borden's popsicles and "fudgsicles" ran a popular television advertisement that began with an old white cowboy telling a group of boys a story in which "injuns, injuns, thousands of 'em swarming all over." With the racial scene established, the advertiser capitalized on the cowboys and Indians scenario when the old cowboy declared, "war paint melted in a great big happy grin" when presented with an Elsie brand popsicle.

44. Yuko Matsukawa, "Representing the Oriental in Nineteenth-Century Trade Cards" in *Re-Collecting Early Asian America: Essays in Cultural History*, eds. Josephine Lee, Imogene L. Lim, and Yuko Matsukawa (Philadelphia: Temple University Press, 2001), 200–201.

45. Ibid., 200–17.

46. *The World's Work* 12 (1906): 7582; T.W.H. Crosland, *The Truth about Japan* (London: Grant Richards, 1904), 4.

47. Esther Forbes, *Paul Revere and the World He Lived in* (New York: Mariner Books, 1999), n. 50, 481.

48. Joan Lee, "Visual Reconnaissance" in *Alien Encounters: Popular Culture in Asian America*, eds. Mimi Thi Nguyen and Thuy Linh Nguyen Tu (Durham, NC: Duke University Press, 2007), 137.

49. Christine B. Balance, "How It Feels to Be Viral Me: Affective Labor and Asian American YouTube Performance" in *Gender, Race, and Class in Media: A Critical Reader*, eds. Gail Dines and Jean M. Humez (4th edition, Thousand Oaks, CA: Sage, 2014), 672.

50. Michael White, *A Short Course in International Marketing Blunders: Mistakes Made by Companies That Should Have Known Better* (Petaluma, CA: World Trade Press, 2001), 139.

51. Oliver Double, *Getting the Joke: The Inner Workings of Stand-Up Comedy* (London: Bloomsbury Publishing, 2005), 225.

52. Anne McClintock, *Imperial Leather: Race, Gender and Sexuality in the Colonial Contest* (New York and London: Routledge, 1995), 32. See also C. Richard King, Carmen R. Lugo-Lugo, and Mary K. Bloodsworth-Lugo, *Animated Difference: Race, Gender, and Sexuality in Contemporary Films for Children* (Lanham, MD: Rowman and Littlefield, 2011), 131.

53. Hoganson, *Consumers' Imperium*, 9, 14.

Chapter 3

1. Jun Xing, *Asian America through the Lens: History, Representations, and Identity* (Lanham, MD: AltaMira Press, 1998), 76; Vincent F. Rocchio, *Reel Racism: Confronting Hollywood's Construction of Afro-American Culture* (Boulder, CO: Westview Press, 2000), 5; Charles R. Berg, *Latino Images in Film: Stereotypes, Subversion, and Resistance* (Austin: University of Texas Press, 2002), 17; Anglea Aleiss, *Making the White Man's Indian: Native Americans and Hollywood Movies* (Santa Barbara, CA: Praeger, 2005), 3, 87, 107, 118.

2. Tania Modleski, *Feminism without Women: Culture and Criticism in a "Postfeminist" Age* (New York and London: Routledge, 1991), 118, 128; Manthia Diawara, "The Blackface Stereotype" in *Blackface*, eds. David Levinthal and Manthia Diawara (Santa Fe, NM: Arena Editions, 1999); Norma Manatu, *African American Women and Sexuality in the Cinema* (Jefferson, NC: McFarland and Company, Inc., 2003), 22.

3. Donald Bogle, *Toms, Coons, Mulattoes, Mammies, and Bucks: An Interpretive History of Blacks in American Films* (New York: Continuum, 1992), 3–4.

4. Patrick McGilligan, *Oscar Micheaux: The Great and Only* (New York: Perennial, 2007).

5. Bogle, *Toms, Coons, Mulattoes, Mammies, and Bucks*, 11.

6. Lee Grieveson, *Policing Cinema: Movies and Censorship in Early-Twentieth-Century America* (Berkeley: University of California Press, 2004), 38.

7. Melvyn Stokes, *The Birth of a Nation: A History of "The Most Controversial Motion Picture of All Time"* (New York: Oxford University Press, 2007), 172.

8. Bogle, *Toms, Coons, Mulattoes, Mammies, and Bucks*, 11–13.

9. Barbara Tepa Lupack, *Literary Adaptations in Black American Cinema: From Micheaux to Morrison* (Rochester, NY: University of Rochester Press, 2002), 209.

10. Bogle, *Toms, Coons, Mulattoes, Mammies, and Bucks*, 89.

11. Helen Taylor, *Scarlett's Women: Gone with the Wind and Its Female Fans* (New Brunswick, NJ: Rutgers University Press, 1989), 169.

12. Bogle, *Toms, Coons, Mulattoes, Mammies, and Bucks*, 92.

13. Cindy Patton, *Cinematic Identity: Anatomy of a Problem Film* (Minneapolis: University of Minnesota Press, 2007), 6.

14. Herbert J. Gans, "The Rise of the Problem-Film: An Analysis of Changes in Hollywood Films and the American Audience," *Social Problems* 11, no. 4 (Spring 1964): 327–28.

15. Angela D. Dillard, *Guess Who's Coming to Dinner Now?: Multicultural Conservatism in America* (New York: New York University Press, 2001), xii.

16. Michele Janette, "Out of the Melting Pot and into the *Frontera*: Race, Sex, Nation, and Home in Velina Hasu Houston's '*American Dreams*' " in *Mixed Race Literature*, ed. Jonathan Brennan (Stanford, CA: Stanford University Press, 2002), 88.

17. John T. Soister, *Up from the Vault: Rare Thrillers of the 1920s and 1930s* (Jefferson, NC: McFarland and Company, Inc., 2004), 3.

18. Thomas Cripps, *Slow Fade to Black: The Negro in American Film, 1900–1942* (New York: Oxford University Press, 1993), 306.

19. Yiman Wang, "The Art of Screen Passing: Anna May Wong's Yellow Yellow-face Performance in the Art Deco Era," *Camera Obscura* 20, no. 3 (2005): 60–159.

20. Daniel J. Kevles, *In the Name of Eugenics: Genetics and the Uses of Human Heredity* (Berkeley: University of California Press, 1985), ix.

21. Lothrop Stoddard, *The Rising Tide of Color against White World-Supremacy* (New York: Charles Scribner's Sons, 1922), 231.

22. Ruth Mayer, "Image Power: Seriality, Iconicity and The Mask of Fu Manchu," *Screen* 53, no. 4 (Winter 2012): 416–17.

23. "Mask of Fu Manchu," http://www.aycyas.com/maskoffumanchu.htm, accessed May 26, 2014.

24. Anthony B. Chan, *Perpetually Cool: The Many Lives of Anna May Wong, 1905–1961* (Lanham, MD: Scarecrow Press, 2003), 116–18; Yunte Huang, *Charlie*

Chan: The Untold Story of the Honorable Detective and His Rendezvous with American History (New York: W.W. Norton and Company, 2010), xv.

25. Ken Hanke, *Charlie Chan at the Movies: History, Filmography, and Criticism* (Jefferson, NC: MacFarland and Company, Inc., 2004), 1.

26. Karla R. Fuller, *Hollywood Goes Oriental: CaucAsian Performance in American Film* (Detroit, MI: Wayne State University Press, 2010), 93.

27. Huang, *Charlie Chan*, 143.

28. Ibid., 266.

29. Hanke, *Charlie Chan at the Movies*, xv.

30. Chan, *Perpetually Cool*, 5–6; Graham Russell Gao Hodges, *Anna May Wong: From Laundryman's Daughter to Hollywood Legend* (Hong Kong: Hong Kong University Press, 2012), 5.

31. Pablo Dominguez Anderson, "'So Tired of the Parts I Had to Play': Anna May Wong and German Orientalism in the Weimar Republic" in *Crossing Boundaries: Ethnicity, Race, and National Belonging in a Transnational World*, eds. Brian D. Behnken and Simon Wendt (Lanham, MD: Lexington Books, 2013), 261–84.

32. Hodges, *Anna May Wong*, 49.

33. Dominguez Anderson, "So Tired of the Parts I Had to Play," 261–84; Hodges, *Anna May Wong*, 86–87; Rishona Zimring, *Social Dance and the Modernist Imagination in Interwar Britain* (Surrey, UK: Ashgate, 2013), 52.

34. Wang, "The Art of Screen Passing."

35. Norman K. Denzin, *Reading Race: Hollywood and the Cinema of Racial Violence* (Thousand Oaks, CA: Sage, 2002), 35–36.

36. David Seed, *Brainwashing: The Fictions of Mind Control: A Study of Novels and Films since World War II* (Kent, OH: Kent State University Press, 2004), 106–7.

37. Fraser A. Sherman, *Screen Enemies of the American Way: Political Paranoia about Nazis, Communists, Saboteurs, Terrorists and Body Snatching Aliens in Film and Television* (Jefferson, NC: McFarland and Company, Inc., 2010), 73–74.

38. Ken Gonzales-Day, *Lynching in the West, 1850–1935* (Durham, NC: Duke University Press, 2006), 184; William Carrigan and Clive Webb, *Forgotten Dead: Mob Violence against Mexicans in the United States, 1848–1928* (New York: Oxford University Press, 2013).

39. Ramón Saldívar, *The Borderlands of Culture: Américo Paredes and the Transnational Imaginary* (Durham, NC: Duke University Press, 2006), 321.

40. Walter N. Burns, *The Robin Hood of El Dorado: The Saga of Joaquin Murrieta, Famous Outlaw of California's Age of Gold* (1932; rpr., Albuquerque: University of New Mexico Press, 1999).

41. Scott L. Baugh, *Latino American Cinema: An Encyclopedia of Movies, Stars, Concepts, and Trends* (Santa Barbara, CA: ABC-CLIO, 2012), 103.

42. Clara E. Rodriguez, *Heroes, Lovers, and Others: The Story of Latinos in Hollywood* (New York: Oxford University Press, 2004), 87–88.

43. Charles Ramírez Berg, *Latino Images in Film: Stereotypes, Subversion, and Resistance* (Austin: University of Texas Press, 2002), 93.

44. Adrián Pérez Melgosa, *Cinema and Inter-American Relations: Tracking Transnational Affect* (New York and Abingdon: Routledge, 2012), 17.

45. R. Philip Loy, *Westerns and American Culture, 1930–1955* (Jefferson, NC: McFarland and Company, Inc., 2001), 209.

46. Michelle Vogel, *Lupe Velez: The Life and Career of Hollywood's Mexican Spitfire* (Jefferson, NC: McFarland and Company, Inc., 2012), 221.

47. France Negron-Muntaner, "Feeling Pretty: West Side Story and Puerto Rican Identity Discourses," *Social Text* 18, no. 2 (Summer 2000): 83–106.

48. Norman L. Zucker and Naomi Flink Zucker, *Desperate Crossings: Seeking Refuge in America* (Armonk, NY: M.E. Sharpe, 1996), 45.

Chapter 4

1. Michael Barrier, *Hollywood Cartoons: American Animation in Its Golden Age* (New York: Oxford University Press, 1999), 404–6.

2. Stefan Kanfer, *Serious Business: The Art and Commerce of Animation in America from Betty Boop to "Toy Story"* (New York: Da Capo Press, 2000), 160.

3. Karl F. Cohen, *Forbidden Animation: Censored Cartoons and Blacklisted Animators in America* (Jefferson, NC: McFarland and Company, Inc., 1997), 55–56; Maureen Furniss, *Art in Motion: Animation Aesthetics* (Sydney: John Libbey and Company, 1998), 232; Michael S. Shull and David E. Wilt, *Doing Their Bit: Wartime American Animated Short Films, 1939–1945* (2nd edition, Jefferson, NC: McFarland and Company, Inc., 2004), 163.

4. On Disney, see Steven Watts, *The Magic Kingdom: Walt Disney and the American Way of Life* (Columbia: University of Missouri Press, 1997); Marc Eliot, *Walt Disney: Hollywood's Dark Prince* (London: Andre Deutsch Ltd, 2003); Henry A. Giroux and Grace Pollock, *The Mouse That Roared: Disney and the End of Innocence* (Lanham, MD: Rowman & Littlefield, 2010); M. Kenneth Booker, *Disney, Pixar, and the Hidden Messages in Children's Film* (Santa Barbara, CA: Greenwood, 2010). On Tex Avery, see Floriane Place-Verghnes, *Tex Avery: A Unique Legacy, 1942–1955* (Eastleigh, UK: John Libbey Publishing, 2006). On general cartoon animators and racism, see Kevin S. Sandler, ed., *Reading the Rabbit: Explorations in Warner Bros. Animation* (Piscataway, NJ: Rutgers University Press, 1998); Christopher P. Lehman, *The Colored Cartoon: Black Representation in American Animated Short Films, 1907–1954* (Amherst: University of Massachusetts Press, 2007); William Anthony Nericco, *Tex{t}-Mex: Seductive Hallucinations of the "Mexican" in America* (Austin: University of Texas Press, 2007).

5. Zoe Burkholder, *Color in the Classroom: How American Schools Taught Race, 1900–1954* (New York: Oxford University Press, 2011), 122, 143; Eric Lott, *Love*

and Theft: Blackface Minstrelsy and the American Working Class (New York: Oxford University Press, 2013), 5.

6. Jeet Heer, "Felix the Cat and Blackface," http://sanseverything.wordpress .com/2009/08/11/felix-the-cat-blackface/.

7. Michael Rogin, *Blackface, White Noise: Jewish Immigrants in the Hollywood Melting Pot* (Berkeley: University of California Press, 1996), 29.

8. As quoted in Nicholas Sammond, "'Who Dat Say Who Dat?' Racial Masquerade, Humor, and the Rise of Modern Animation" in *Funny Pictures: Animation and Comedy in Studio-Rea Hollywood*, eds. Daniel Goldmark and Charlie Keil (Berkeley: University of California Press, 2011), 142.

9. Dating back to at least the mid-nineteenth century, the phrase "Tar Heels" has been used as the nickname of North Carolina. The origins of the term remain shrouded in uncertainty, with some suggesting that it references North Carolina's tar and turpentine production; other than that, it has more sinister, possibly, racist, origins. For further analysis, see Walt Wolfram and Jeffrey Reaser, *Talkin' Tar Heel: How Our Voices Tell the Story of North Carolina* (Chapel Hill: University of North Carolina Press, 2014), 4–6.

10. Terry Lindvall and Ben Fraser, "Darker Shades of Animation: African-American Images in the Warner Bros. Cartoon" in *Reading the Rabbit: Explorations in Warner Bros. Animation*, ed. Kevin Sandler (New Brunswick, NJ: Rutgers University Press 1998), 125.

11. Timothy S. Susanin, *Walt before Mickey: Disney's Early Years, 1919–1928* (Jackson: University of Mississippi Press, 2011), 103.

12. Anthony Balducci, *The Funny Parts: A History of Film Routines and Gags* (Jefferson, NC: McFarland and Company, Inc., 2012), 256–58.

13. Michael Barrier, *The Animated Man: A Life of Walt Disney* (Berkeley: University of California Press, 2007), 50–51.

14. Ibid., 322; Carter A. Wilson, *Racism: From Slavery to Advanced Capitalism* (Thousand Oaks, CA: Sage Publications, 1996), 112.

15. Nicholas Sammond, "'Gentlemen, Please Be Seated': Racial Masquerade and Sadomasochism in 1930s Animation" in *Burnt Cork: Traditions and Legacies of Blackface Minstrelsy*, ed. Stephen Johnson (Amherst: University of Massachusetts Press, 2012), 164.

16. Paul Wells, *Understanding Animation* (New York and London: Routledge, 1998), 74.

17. The same motif appeared in the first cartoon to feature the character "Popeye," who made his debut in the *Betty Boop* short "Popeye the Sailor."

18. J. Emmett Winn, *Documenting Racism: African Americans in U.S. Department of Agriculture Documentaries, 1921–42* (New York: Continuum, 2012), 23.

19. Wells, *Understanding Animation*, 74.

20. Kanfer, *Serious Business*, 160.

21. Thomas Pluck, "Redemption for Mammy Two Shoes," March 4, 2009, http://thomaspluck.com/2009/03/04/redemption-for-mammy-Two   Shoes/,

accessed April 3, 2014. On the wages of whiteness, see David R. Roediger, *Wages of Whiteness: Race and the Making of the American Working Class* (New York: Verso, 1991).

22. Michael S. Shull and David E. Wilt, *Doing Their Bit: Wartime American Animated Short Films, 1939–1945* (Jefferson, NC: McFarland & Company Inc. Publishers, 2004), 62.

23. See, for example, Brenda J. Child, *Boarding School Seasons: American Indian Families, 1900–1940* (Lincoln: University of Nebraska Press, 1998).

24. On the Plains, and in the American West generally, Native Americans and cowboys routinely provided aid to each other. The true antagonists to Native American communities were federal troops. See Devon Abbott Mihesuah, *American Indians: Stereotypes and Realities* (Atlanta, GA: Clarity Press, 2013).

25. See Arnoldo De León, *They Called Them Greasers: Anglo Attitudes toward Mexicans in Texas, 1821–1900* (Austin: University of Texas Press, 1983); David J. Weber, *Myth and History of the Hispanic Southwest* (Albuquerque: University of New Mexico Press, 1988).

26. AAP also developed shorts such as Popeye.

27. See Karl F. Cohen, *Forbidden Animation: Censored Cartoons and Blacklisted Animators in America* (Jefferson, NC: McFarland and Company, Inc., 1997).

28. Lindvall and Fraser, "Darker Shades of Animation," 128.

29. Christopher P. Lehman, *The Colored Cartoon: Black Representation in American Animated Short Films, 1907–1954* (Amherst: University of Massachusetts Press, 2007), 78–79.

30. Sandler, *Reading the Rabbit*, 11.

31. Shull and Wilt, *Doing Their Bit*, 38.

32. Cohen, *Forbidden Animation*, 59.

33. Eileen Welsome, *The General and the Jaguar: Pershing's Hunt for Pancho Villa: A True Story of Revolution and Revenge* (New York: Little, Brown, and Company, 2006), 108–12; Sherry L. Meinberg, *The Cockroach Invasion* (Bloomington, IN: Archway Publishing, 2014), 99.

34. For an excellent commentary on Speedy Gonzales, see Nericcio, *Tex{t}-Mex*, 125–33. The Cartoon Network began re-airing old *Speedy Gonzales* cartoons in 2003. See Steven Bender, *Greasers and Gringos: Latinos, Law, and the American Imagination* (New York: New York University Press, 2003), 65.

35. On this point, see Jenny Woodley, *Art of Equality: The NAACP's Cultural Campaign for Civil Rights* (Lexington: University Press of Kentucky, 2014).

Conclusion

1. Martha Biondi, *To Stand and Fight: The Struggle for Civil Rights in Postwar New York City* (Cambridge, MA: Harvard University Press, 2003), 95–96.

2. William N. Thompson, *Native American Issues: A Reference Handbook* (Santa Barbara, CA: ABC-CLIO, 2005), 285.

3. Daniel Bernadi, "Blacks in Early Cinema" in *African Americans and Popular Culture*, ed. Todd Boyd (volume 1: Westport, CT: Greenwood Publishing Group, 2008), 29.

4. Whoopi Goldberg commentary, https://www.youtube.com/watch?v=k_oEOdIBOpU, accessed August 30, 2014.

5. Chon A. Noriega, *Shot in America: Television, the State, and the Rise of Chicano Cinema* (Minneapolis: University of Minnesota Press, 2000), 40–42.

6. "Press Release," by Albert Peña Jr., July 22, 1968, Judge Albert A. Peña Papers, Special Collections, University of Texas, San Antonio.

7. Noriega, *Shot in America*, 42.

8. "Pena Aims Heavy Guns at Image Distortion," *The Sun*, August 22, 1968.

9. "The True Image of the Mexican-American," IMAGE statement, January 18, 1969, in Peña Papers.

10. "Adios Bandito," *Texas Monthly*, January 1986.

11. Steven Salaita, "Nothing Scarier Than a Nervous White Man: The 'Redskins' Debate Is Really about White Privilege," *Salon*, http://www.salon.com/2013/09/29/nothing_scarier_than_a_nervous_white_man_the_redskins_debate_is_really_about_white_privilege/, accessed August 30, 2014.

12. Gregory D. Smithers, "The Soul of Unity: The Quarterly Journal of the Society of American Indians, 1913–1915," *American Indian Quarterly* 37, no. 3 (Summer 2013): 269.

13. Rayna Green, "The Tribe Called Wannabe: Playing Indian in America and Europe," *Folklore* 99, no. 1 (1988): 30–55; Jason Edward Black, "The 'Mascotting' of Native America: Construction, Commodity, and Assimilation," *American Indian Quarterly* 26, no. 4 (Autumn 2002): 606–7.

14. For the "Change the Mascot" campaign, see http://www.changethemascot.org/, accessed August 28, 2014.

15. Michael Martinez, "A Slur or a Term of 'Honor'? Controversy Heightens about Washington Redskins," CNN, October 12, 2013, http://www.cnn.com/2013/10/12/us/redskins-controversy/, accessed August 30, 2014.

16. Carol Cornelius, *Iroquois Corn in a Culture-Based Curriculum: A Framework for Respectfully Teaching about Cultures* (Albany, NY: SUNY Press, 1999), 6–7.

Index

About the Authors

Brian D. Behnken is associate professor in the Department of History and the U.S. Latino/a Studies Program at Iowa State University. He is the author of the book, *Fighting Their Own Battles: Mexican Americans, African Americans, and the Struggle for Civil Rights in Texas,* and two edited volumes, *The Struggle in Black and Brown: African American and Mexican American Relations during the Civil Rights Era* and *Crossing Boundaries: Ethnicity, Race, and National Belonging in a Transnational World.*

Gregory D. Smithers is associate professor of history at Virginia Commonwealth University. He is the author of numerous books and articles on race and racism. His most recent book is *The Cherokee Diaspora.*

CPSIA information can be obtained
at www.ICGtesting.com
Printed in the USA
LVHW061146310722
724794LV00014B/41